A Tongue in the Sink

Denny Fried

A Tongue in the Sink

The Harrowing Adventures of a
Baby Boomer Childhood

Dennis Fried, Ph.D.

Eiffel Press

ISBN: 0-9679335-1-X
Library of Congress Control Number: 2003095275

Book design and production: Tabby House
Drawing on p. 11: Barry Hopkins
Manufactured in the United States of America
First printing: January 2004

This is a work of nonfiction; however, some names
have been changed to protect the guilty.

Eiffel Press
P.O. Box 339
Osprey, FL 34229
www.eiffelpress.net

In memory of good friends lost to time.

Contents

Looking west over the Hudson River and the Rip Van Winkle Bridge toward the Catskill Mountains.

1

Got a Minute?

Comparing life to a journey is a well-worn cliché. Yet, for me, there's an ironic difference between the two that makes it less than a happy analogy. When traveling by car or plane, for instance, the closer I get to my destination, the more I find myself thinking about where I'm going. In life, the closer I get to my final port of call, the more time I spend reflecting on where I've been.

If you ask me (and even if you don't), where I've been was a better time and place than where I am.

Where I am is third-millennium Florida, a spectacular show-case for the human obsession to replace the natural world with an inferior, man-made version. Walt Disney came to the right place.

Examples abound. Innumerable acres of Florida wetlands, nature's environmental regulators, have been developed out of existence so that Wal-Marts and Home Depots might flourish. As a result, storm water, with no place left to run, now seeks refuge in the living rooms of cookie-cutter developments with names like Pelican Point and Palm-Air. (The letter 'e' is one of the most expensive residential upgrades available in Florida. A house in Pelican Point valued at $200,000 would sell for $425,000 in Pelican Pointe.)

In fact, Florida developers are nothing less than semantical wizards—they have managed to convince thousands of homeowners that drainage ditches are actually lakes. And what would you think about buying a house that abuts a sterile field, upon which noxious chemicals are periodically dumped, and over which hordes of people dressed in nightmarish pastels march all day and evening long, launching potentially lethal projectiles? Congratulations, you've just paid an extra hundred grand for a *golf course home*.

Aside from decorative palms, which must be propped up with boards and wire to keep them from falling over during storms, trees are not welcome in Florida because they tend to get in the way of the most prevalent driver group here: those who have lost control of their vehicles. Even more noteworthy is that drivers here who are members of this group are rarely aware of it. It's quite common to pick up the morning paper and see a photograph of a car parked in the middle of someone's kitchen, or a restaurant, or the bay. The standard explanation for such accidents is that the unfortunate drivers confused the brake and the accelerator, something they obviously didn't notice until they had careened fifty yards, bombed over a curb, and busted through a wall or a guardrail.

All this is less than comforting when sitting in your car at a red light (which here in Florida functions only as a polite suggestion); almost everyone I know has been rear-ended while doing so. It happened to me a couple of years ago. I was in a line of cars stopped at a light, it turned green, and before the cars in front of me had a chance to move I was slammed from behind so hard that my car hit the one in front of me, and that car hit the one in front of it. The explanation? A woman two cars behind me saw the light turn green and took off, despite the fact that the line of cars in front of her had not yet done so.

Have you ever driven by the scene of a fender-bender and seen the participants calmly discussing the situation? That wasn't me.

Some of our road warriors get a little too playful on the highways. Recently a local motorcycle gang was making its usual weekend tavern tour when one member decided to stretch his legs and stand up in the saddle while going sixty miles an hour. He dutifully fell off the bike and suffered brain damage, though it's hard to see how that's possible. Meanwhile his bike continued down the road, picking up speed from the suddenly lighter load, until it veered off into a parking lot and struck a car. When interviewed on local TV, one of the injured man's grief-stricken colleagues solemnly reported, "I knew something was wrong when I saw his bike come by without him."

Aside from being a menace to traffic, trees are also messy and drop stuff on lawns, natural stuff such as leaves and twigs. Lawns, being as unnatural as a concise politician, do not look good with leaves and twigs on them.

I used to think that the best and quickest way to learn about people was to peruse their bookshelves. A good alternative, and one which does not require admission into the home, is to study their lawns. During my college-teaching days, I used to jog through an expensive neighborhood whose homes were owned mostly by high-priced bureaucrats whose job was to administrate us low-priced professors. Every yard was beautifully landscaped and meticulously manicured, but one stood out from all the rest: the grass was a smidge greener, the flowers a little brighter, the bushes a bit shapelier.

But more than this, I came to realize that I had never seen one tiny bit of foreign matter on the lawn—not a twig, not a leaf, not to mention not a dog turd. Even in the fall, when leaves were blowing like snowflakes, the yard remained pristine as if protected by some horticultural force field. I seriously wondered whether someone sat at the window all day and ran out immediately to clear away any aesthetic insults.

Then one afternoon, while jogging by, I was stunned into motionlessness. There, in the middle of the lawn, lay a solitary brown leaf. I couldn't believe it. I considered going back to the house to get my camera to photograph this spectacle and blackmail the residents. I continued my run, wondering at what I had just seen.

But, fifteen minutes later, when I passed by the yard again on my return trip, the leaf was gone. (And, I could never quite resolve the question of whether I was happy or disturbed by this.)

Most people consider a virgin forest, in all its wildness, to be beautiful. But take a piece of that same forest and make it your yard, and in ten minutes your neighbors would be massing like the Frankenstein posse. *Remove that horror and plant a lawn, for God's sake!*

Wild animals, like trees, are really up against it in Florida. Consider the poor alligators: they retired to Florida 50,000,000 years before humans were even a twinkle in the monkey's eye. This impressive heritage entitles them to a bullet in the head whenever their reptilian dating instincts lead them to areas where they can be seen by humans who haven't bought a ticket for the privilege.

This blowing away of animals comes under the rubric of wildlife management, which is very big in Florida. It's hard not to feel sorry for all these animals who can't *manage* themselves without human intervention, and it makes you wonder why the Department of Natural Resources wasn't created right along with the animals to begin with.

However, not all of Florida's downside can be blamed on the hand (or bulldozer) of man; for example, there's the danger inherent in the weather. For six months every year, we Floridians get to watch the randomness of fate played out on the weather map, as hurricanes are fired at us like bullets from a warped musket. Deciding whether to flee or not in the face of an approaching storm is a very popular parlor game down here. In truth, it probably matters very little which choice you make. If the storm is not a bad one, you'll come out fine in either case.

If, on the other hand, a big one has its eye on you, you can fly away in the comfort of your own home, or in your car (which undoubtedly will have gotten stuck in a massive traffic jam only a few miles from where you used to live). First class or coach, the choice is yours.

So why am I here? I'm glad I asked. I'm in Florida because, after more than forty northern winters, frostbite of the extremities has lost its *je ne sais quoi*. Why was I voluntarily living in a place where for six months a year, if I took a lawn chair and sat out in my yard, within thirty minutes I'd be dead? So in the winter of 1990, I threw all my worldly possessions into the back of my (very small) car and headed for the Sunshine State. (I was very proud of the fact that, even in my mid-forties, I could still fit everything I owned into my car. It was a tremendous source of comfort to know that any time I got pissed off or pissed on enough, I could vanish without a clue by morning. Understand, I never actually did this—I always left a note and called it a career change.)

I settled in Sarasota, on the Gulf Coast, known to me from family vacations taken in the 1950s. It was, for the most part, unrecognizable because of the enhanced quality of life an additional 300,000 people and their automobiles add to what is essentially a small town.

On the very day I arrived, as if on a pilgrimage, I went to look for the "motor court" where I had stayed so many times four decades earlier. Considering how much the town had changed, I held out little hope that it had survived. But there it was, as if suspended in time: same name, same shuffleboard court, same rickety little pavilion that sheltered a Coke machine and a Ping-Pong table. I took a nostalgic walk around the grounds, and I was ambushed by tears. I imagined that if I closed my eyes and concentrated intensely enough, I would be able to hear my own childhood laughter still echoing there.

Thus I became one of the thousand people a day who move to Florida in search of a warmer, if not better, life. The next challenge was finding a legal way to earn money. Scam artists do very well down here, purportedly because of the large elderly population. Personally, I've never been able to figure out the essential connection between being old and being willing to pay two strangers with no teeth $25,000 to seal a driveway. But that's just me.

Florida is primarily a service economy. This means you're either a rich person or you're cutting a rich person's grass. Having been a nuclear physicist and then a philosophy professor in earlier years, I had no skills that anyone was willing to pay for.

So in the face of economic challenge, I took a page from corporate America and restructured myself: I became computer literate. Traditionally, a literate person is one who reads easily, writes with grace, and manipulates concepts with a respectable degree of logical precision. Few such people still exist, which is just as well because they tend to be liberals.

Today it is absolutely essential to be computer literate. Computer literacy enables you to cruise the Internet and spend hours typing to people you wouldn't have anything to do with if they were standing right next to you. It empowers you to run a spreadsheet to compose your weekly shopping list. It also teaches one of the most noble of all the human virtues, patience, in that you learn not to hurl your computer against the nearest hard surface, when every synapse in your body is firing away in the desperate attempt to make you do so.

Armed with my newly acquired, cutting-edge skills, I soon found employment with a software development company. The advances in software have been absolutely critical to the technological revolution which has transformed our world in the last two decades. I don't have this on tape, but I'm quite sure the business meeting in which the concept of software was first discussed went like this:

18

Company president: "We are going broke. Our machines are unreliable, our complaint lines are burning up, and covering the warranty repairs is killing us. We've got to do something."

Marketing Whiz #1: "If only we could pin the blame on someone else. You know, like if only we could get away with saying that our machines contain an invisible fairy dust made by mystical beings who are very hard to contact, and that there's nothing wrong with our product—it has to be the fairy dust that's screwed up."

Company president: "Who in hell promoted you to court jester?"

Marketing Whiz #2: "Wait a minute, Boss. I think he's on to something here. Only instead of "fairy dust" we'll just call it....

Marketing Whiz #1: "Software!"

My new job was to sit in front of a computer all day and test the fairy dust by clicking at things. I also taught our customers what to click at, and I wrote manuals that described the difference between good clicks and bad ones.

This was a typical New Economy job, in that it paid well and was completely lethal to long-term mental health. To get through the day, I would sometimes gaze out the window at the palm-lined parking lots and reminisce about the beginning of my journey, a time and place lost in reality but preserved in memory. A healthier time and place, it seems to me now.

But don't take my word for it. Come back with me for a brief visit. Judge for yourself.

2

The Land of Rip-Off Van Winkle

Most people, at one time or another, try to imagine what it's like to be dead. In fact, this is a very easy thing to do. Just think back to how it felt before you were born and you've got it.

I was in that very condition until June 29, 1946, when I became one of the first shots squeezed off in what eventually became known as the "baby boom." I held my fire as long as I could, though—my mother was in labor so long that the doctor began to fear for both our lives. I suspect that somewhere in my prepartum subconscious lurked the realization that the sooner I made my appearance, the sooner I would have to start school.

But at last I surrendered and showed my face for the very first time in a small town in upstate New York called Catskill. For those unfamiliar with the geography of New York, upstate New York encompasses everything north of Saks Fifth Avenue. This area is also referred to as the "sticks," the "boonies," or the "country." (The proper term depends on the context. A New York City resident considers the unfortunate inhabitants of that remote region to be from the "sticks" or the "boonies." On the other hand, his own weekend retreat is said to be in the "country.")

So, to be more specific, Catskill is on the west bank of the Hudson River, about 120 miles north of Saks Fifth Avenue.

Most people think of the Catskills as "the place where all the big Jewish hotels are," sometimes also referred to as "the Jewish Alps" (an oxymoron on par with "Nazi delicatessen"). In fact, they're thinking of Sullivan County, about seventy miles southwest of Catskill (which lies in Greene County). Most of the Jewish hotels there are gone now, burned to the ground (some accidentally) or taken over by weird religious sects that spend a lot of time in airports without going anywhere.

The town of Catskill itself is in the Hudson Valley, with the mountains dominating the view to the west. From Catskill you drive for about fifteen minutes before starting to ascend a winding, narrow, two-lane road with exquisite heights blocking out the sun above, and drop-offs into misty gorges mere feet from your tires. On the hottest summer day, when the heat and humidity in the valley are unrelenting, the air in that pass has an autumn bite to it.

Many of the people who live in those mountains are as hillbilly as anyone you're likely to find in Kentucky or West Virginia. Families live in the same house for generations, talk with a mountain twang, are known to cook up a little shine when necessary, and don't much cotton to strangers. They have more appliances outdoors than the average wealthy family has indoors, and every car that they or their ancestors ever owned is born again as a chicken coop.

A number of years ago an incident occurred in one of those small mountain towns that neatly sums up the spirit of the place. Seems that a feller harbored a grudge ginst someone, and one night he picked up his shotgun and went into town lookin for im. He found the mangy varmint walkin on the street, put the gun back of his head and pushed im face up ginst a buildin, and there they stayed for a good long while as the gun-toter ranted and raved and onlookers gawked, fraid to do notin.

Well, news travels fast in a small mountain town, and it weren't too long afore the victim's brother caught wind of the affair and grabbed his shotgun and went into town his own damn self. When he reached the scene he pushed his way through the crowd and placed his gun to the back of the head of the gun-toter. And there they stayed, no one daring to move, as perfect an illustration of balance of power as you are ever likely to see.

Eventually the state police arrived—most of these towns are too small to have their own police force—and after a lengthy negotiation were able to defuse the confrontation and confiscate the guns. The two Wyatt Earps spent the night in jail, eventually paid a small fine, and that was that. Nobody had gotten hurt and, after all, men will sometimes be boys.

In reality, the Catskill area's one enduring claim to fame is that it was the home of Rip Van Winkle. Rip Van Winkle, by way of reminder, was that old Dutchman who wandered out into the woods with a flask one day, had trouble holding his liquor, and fell asleep for a few decades. When he awoke, he had an incredibly long white beard full of spiders and could only recall watching a bowling dwarf toss a perfect game with a ball so powerful that it sounded like thunder every time it hit the 1-3 pocket. He made his way back home, trying to think of an excuse that would wash, but he lucked out because by that time his wife was dead, and so were all his neighbors.

Catskillians find this story so inspirational that they feel compelled to name everything in sight after this legendary character. The Rip Van Winkle Bridge takes you west across the Hudson River right into Catskill proper. You can immediately fill your gas tank at the Rip Van Winkle Service Station, have lunch at the Rip Van Winkle Diner, wash your clothes at the Rip Van Winkle Laundromat, dine at the Rip Van Winkle Tavern, then bowl a few games at the Rip Van Winkle Lanes. (The lane that the dwarf used for his perfect game was removed from the mountains in 1952 and is now on permanent display at the Bowling Hall of Fame in Akron, Ohio). And, of course, sleep for a few nights, or decades, in the Rip Van Winkle Motel.

The residents of Catskill when I was growing up there numbered about 5000, and the general population was so poor that both sides of the track were wrong. There was one stoplight in the entire town, at the intersection of Main and Bridge streets. Main Street was the principal thoroughfare and the primary shopping area for the entire county. Bridge Street crossed over the Catskill Creek by way of a—you figure it out for yourself. Then there was Maple Avenue (lots of pretty trees), Broad Street (extremely wide), Church Street (the place to be on Sunday morning), and Grandview Avenue (a beautiful vista of the Hudson River). This sort of thing is ample illustration of the propensity of human beings to look on the bright side. Were it otherwise, small towns everywhere would sport street names like Horseshit Promenade, Mudhole Lane, and Stinkwater Boulevard.

***

The bulk of what meager employment there was in the area was manual labor provided by the railroad, a truck-body manufacturer, and a couple of cement plants situated on the river about five miles south of Catskill in a hamlet with a name that pulled no punches: Cementon. (Cementon was as dreary a place as you can imagine: drab little wooden houses; steep streets riddled with potholes; and everything in sight blanketed with cement dust, so that it always seemed that one good rain would convert the entire town into a collection of very large lawn ornaments.)

But for two months each year, from the Fourth of July to Labor Day, there was another source of revenue: the "boarders." The boarders flocked up from assorted hellholes such as Bwooklyn and New Joisey and actually created weekend traffic jams on Main Street. They also jammed up the sidewalks, since boarder families insisted on walking all abreast in a flying wedge. To get around them we had to time it just right and pirouette around a parking meter.

These boarders were so called because they stayed in boarding houses, which invariably consisted of individual bungalow units, a main house containing a recreation room and dining hall, a concrete swimming pool, a horseshoe pit, and a softball field. If the resort was Italian, as many were, there was also a bocci court. (The rules of bocci are complex, but they essentially require that you drink beer all afternoon long, insult the genetic origins of all fellow players, and occasionally drop a ball on the ground.)

Male Italian boarders were all named Louis (pronounced "Looey"), had hairy chests, and wore a minimum of three gold chains at a time. Whenever a parent screamed "Looey!" thirty-four kids would come running. The women were all named Maria, chewed gum, and snapped it.

Italian men and women had absolutely nothing to do with one another, at least in public. The men talked and laughed among themselves, occasionally collaring a passing child in order to torture it by pinching its cheek, while the women gathered in their own group and attempted to ascertain whose husband was the biggest asshole. The children threw ice at one another and rubbed their aching cheeks.

In addition to the Italians, there was also a large contingent of Irish boarders, many from the Boston area. In fact, there was a small town about five miles from Catskill named Leeds, and it was renowned throughout the northeast as an "Irish center." Leeds consisted of a general store, a diner, a Catholic church, and ten bars, thus providing a perfect example of a socially engineered community, inadvertent though it was.

For ten months of the year you could nap undisturbed in the middle of Leeds's one and only street, a luxury commonly enjoyed by residents who left the bars after a night of drinking only to discover that their houses were not where they had left them. But during high summer (literally speaking), especially on Friday and Saturday nights, pedestrians had to dodge cars even on the sidewalks. No tourist season was complete without at least one Irish boarder being dispatched to his own wake by a car. (Also, there was always at least one drowning in the area, invariably an Italian boarder named Louis. The causes for this ethnic specialization are open to hypothesis.)

The largest and most popular bar in Leeds was O'Shea's, a rambling, two-story wooden structure that housed a huge beer hall at street-level and rooms for rent on the second floor. On summer nights the place was vibrant with live Gaelic music, dancing, laughter, and the spice of the Irish brogue sprinkled throughout. It was an intersection of time and place that made you smile just to be there.

Many of the waiters and waitresses were young students from Ireland who worked for the summer in return for room, board, and abuse from the patrons. They were fresh faced, rosy cheeked, and hard to understand. But they did have exotic ways of turning a phrase. I once asked a waiter what the weather was like in Ireland during the winter:

"In the morning and in the afternoon it's not so bad," he sing-songed, "but in the evening it gets cold enough to freeze the balls off a brass monkey, I swear it."

This was novel stuff for those of us who had never experienced temperatures colder than a witch's tit.

The most popular night at O'Shea's was Wednesday, because that's when the weekly amateur hour was held. The show was supposed to start at 10:00 P.M., and by 9:30 the place would be packed with hundreds of people chugging beer and knocking down shots, getting into a serious talent-judging disposition. But Jerry O'Shea was no fool. He knew that just as soon as amateur hour was over his paying customers would stampede for the front door, leaving behind little more than an indoor toxic waste dump and a smattering of inert figures slumped over tables and chairs.

So every Wednesday night the show would be "delayed" later and later, until the masses started stamping their feet and rhythmically slamming their mugs down on the tables and bar. And then, mere seconds before mob violence broke out, Jerry O'Shea would bound onto the stage and start the show. A master of timing was Jerry O'Shea.

The acts normally included several traditional step dance routines and at least four renditions of "Danny Boy." The dancers were usually good, and the singers invariably horrendous. When all the contestants had finished, they got up on stage side by side, and Jerry O'Shea himself would walk the line and, pointing to one act at a time, call for applause. The winners were determined by sheer noise level. As far as I can remember, they won absolutely nothing.

The skillful dancers never had a chance. For the whole purpose of amateur hour was to enjoy watching people voluntarily degrade themselves in public, preferably to the strains of "Danny Boy." The worse the performance, the more raucous the shrieks and applause that greeted it.

On one momentous occasion a young stranger showed up with a guitar case, and the anticipation began to build. No one in memory had attempted to play an instrument in amateur hour before, and the exciting prospect of watching some innocent, earnest folk singer fall totally apart in front of hundreds of hysterical drunks was almost too much to bear.

When the young man's turn finally arrived, he walked across the room and sat on the edge of the stage. You could have heard a shotglass drop. And then he began to play and sing, and he was absolutely magnificent. The crowd was stunned by this cruel twist of fate. For about thirty seconds the hope persisted that by a miraculous reversal of fortune his voice would break and chords would get slaughtered and we would finally be treated to the level of performance we so truly deserved.

It never happened. By the middle of the song everyone was totally ignoring the young man on stage, who might as well have become invisible. He was a traitor to the cause and merited no better. And when it came time for the judging, the undisputed winner was a little old lady of about eighty who had brought down the house with an unreasonable facsimile of "When Irish Eyes Are Smiling," generated in a voice reminiscent of a chainsaw hitting a spike. The folk singer received the barest whisper of applause. Some say there was the hint of a smile on his face as he packed up his guitar and silently slipped into the night. To my knowledge he was never seen in Leeds again.

***

Labor Day was the grand finale to the summer tourist season. There was a final orgy of block parties, festivals, and picnics. The smell of hops and hot dogs permeated the air, and broken bottles littered the roads. Then the exodus began. The boarding houses closed down, people stopped drowning and getting hit by cars, and we could walk down the sidewalk on a Friday night without having to leapfrog entire families speaking some unidentifiable urban variant of English. We could also yell "Looey!" without anyone giving a damn.

For the following two months, as the air became crisp and the leaves began to jump ship, the area was once again solidly in the hands of the locals. All was right in our little, insular refuge from civilization. Until November. Then we were invaded once again, but this time by tourists of a different stripe: the hunters.

Once upon a time, hunting had an inescapable logic to it— find and kill something to eat or buy the farm. But one day a discovery was made that forever altered the course of human development—supermarkets! And suddenly the man of the house could spend his weekends watching sports on TV instead of crawling around a hostile environment trying to turn out the lights on one of God's creatures.

But there persists an element of the population that is unable to ignore the call of the wild. Surviving on little more than cigarettes and beer, these warriors comb the woods for days on end with modern high-tech weapons, searching for something, anything, to shoot at.

The majority of the hunters invading the Catskills each season hailed from wilderness outposts such as Hackensack. They came to shoot deer, but the fact was that a deer was relatively safe so long as there was a cow, dog, or another hunter in the area. Out of desperation some local farmers actually took to painting their barnyard animals in bright primary colors. But this had little protective effect because many hunters apparently assumed that this was a sneaky adaptive mechanism on the part of the deer, and they were not about to be fooled by it.

With amazing frequency the hunters even shot themselves. They shot themselves climbing over fences, falling out of trees, and proving to their buddies that their guns were empty. They also broke assorted bones tripping over brush, suffered hypothermia from the chilly autumn rains, and experienced heart attacks while dragging their own impressive bulk over the hilly countryside.

And some deer did manage to get themselves shot. These unfortunates, who only hours before had been bounding through the woods with the grace of the wind, now found themselves tied to the hoods of Fords, tongues hanging from blood-smeared mouths and eyes wide open as if to say, "Ain't this a bitch." And down the highways they went, headed for Hackensack.

***

So the seasons and the boarders and the hunters came and went, while the local population stayed put and intermarried. In fact, the ethnic makeup of Catskillians mirrored very closely that of the boarders, with a high proportion of Italians and Irish. There was also a sizeable contingent of "colored people." Nowadays, of course, that term is taken as an insult, just as to call someone "a Black" in those days would have been an invitation to mayhem. Like fashions, insults come and go.

That Catskill had any Black residents at all made it unique in the local rural area. The cities of Albany to the north and Kingston to the south had large Black populations, but the small towns and villages in between were as white as a Republican cocktail party. Except for Catskill.

The Blacks in Catskill lived in one confined area, a wooded dale in the middle of town called Willard's Alley. Willard's Alley was a bit of the old South that had somehow been uprooted and transplanted in the middle of New York. The unpainted wooden houses were mostly one-story structures with shaky porches and tar-paper roofs. The roads were dirt and became quagmires during hard rains. The smell of wood smoke and kerosene hung heavy over Willard's Alley through the cold days of winter, and dogs barked and roosters crowed all year round.

Racial tension was nearly absent in our little world. Schoolyard fighting was an equal opportunity endeavor: everybody argued and fought with everybody, just the way it should be. Nobody scrapped over skin color because of the many more important issues to be resolved, such as whether or not the tag had been made in time at second base, or whether someone's sister really had screwed that flea-bitten donkey over at Farmer Culbertson's.

Sometimes we picked teams by skin color, but that was only because it was quicker and easier than deciding on two captains, choosing to see who would pick first, and then taking turns selecting the players until it got down to the last few nobody wanted. (There is no feeling in life quite like getting picked last on the playground. It stays with you forever. You can grow up to be the toughest sonofabitch in the valley, a titan of big business, the President of the United States. It doesn't matter. Because in your heart, you know you're still the same schmuck who got picked last on a windy sandlot in 1955.)

"Boots against the paddies," someone would yell. Blacks against the whites. Instantaneous teams with built-in uniforms. Could that be the reason for the evolution of different races?

We were all friends, enemies, teammates, rivals. And yet, few white people dared enter Willard's Alley alone. It was as if the world that we understood ended where that dirt road began. Almost every kid knew someone who knew someone who had ventured into Willard's Alley by himself and never been seen again. No dates, never any names. But someone, sometime. I swear to God.

In the mid-1950s the town authorities moved the residents of Willard's Alley into "the project," a collection of newly-built row houses on the Catskill Creek. Bulldozers steamed into Willard's Alley and flattened everything, trees and houses alike. I remember standing on a nearby hillside and watching as the old shacks rose up as if in a final salute, twist into odd angles, and then fall in a cloud of dust. If the authorities found signs of all the people who had disappeared in there, they weren't saying.

A municipal parking lot was constructed where Willard's Alley once stood. Now, for a nickel an hour, white people could place their tread where once they had feared to trod.

3

My Family

I grew up in a second-story apartment on Main Street, the heart of town. For the first three years of my life I was forced to share this space with my mother and father. Then things got even worse with the arrival of my baby brother, Randy.

My father, Stanford, was a dentist and had his office in the front part of the building, while our apartment was in the rear. The wall separating the office and our apartment was obviously not up to the task, because through it we could hear all the cries and screams issuing from my father's satisfied customers. This could explain why, when adults asked me if I wanted to be a dentist just like my dad (which they always did), I told them no. I was going to be a cowboy. A jet pilot. Maybe a contract killer. But definitely not a dentist.

An adult's perspective on the world is skewed by what he sells. To a shoe salesman, you are essentially a human shoetree. To a barber, you're little more than a bad haircut. To my father, you were a set of teeth in need of some serious drilling.

He was obsessed with the Platonic ideal of teeth: white, nicely shaped, lined up like kernels on a prize-winning ear of corn. My teeth came in like the oral equivalent of a drunken stagger. My father took this to be his punishment for some long forgotten sin.

33

But I was the one who had to pay the price, because I was the one who had to wear braces. I've done no research on this, but I'm certain the origin of braces can be traced back to the Inquisition. They cut my lips (and those of my girlfriend) and made my breath stink. I had to avoid any food that tasted good. They made me the object of ridicule. And every few weeks I had to go back so the orthodontist could literally *tighten the screws* on me.

And after four years of this torture, when the braces were finally removed, my nearly straight teeth scrambled back to their original positions virtually overnight.

Please—if you have a child and his teeth are coming out of his nose, by all means consider braces. Otherwise, find some other way to torment the poor bastard.

My father had a weak spot for the underdog. Though highly educated, he often seemed to prefer the company of those whose honest relationship to the world had not been fogged up by an overabundance of intellectual concepts.

He hated dressing up, couldn't stand "parties" where people wandered around with drinks in their hands, mining for witty conversation.

He did enjoy playing cards, and once a week Irving, the local baker, came to our house to play gin. Irving looked like he ate everything he didn't sell, and he constantly chewed on an unlit cigar, which stank up the house anyway.

As soon as Irving left, we'd make our father tell us how much he had lost, and then he would begin his weekly litany about how Irving didn't know a damned thing about gin, but was the luckiest person he had ever seen in his life. This went on for years.

My father's concepts and opinions did not come in shades of gray. There were two ways to do anything: the right way and the wrong way. There were two kinds of people: good ones and bad ones. There was one thing to do with a commitment: keep it.

His moral code was straightforward: live and let live, unless someone threatened his or his family's humanity. In that case, all bets were off. He was gentle and soft-spoken, until someone crossed a line which he seemed to have firmly drawn in his mind. Then even violence was a possibility.

I saw this line crossed only once. I played basketball in junior high, and after a game one very cold winter night I found that a janitor had locked one of the hallway gates, blocking my access to a locker in which I had stored my coat and gloves before the game.

I went back into the gym and found Bill, the janitor on duty that evening. Bill was a nasty prick who was hated by most everyone. I apologetically told him my story, that the gate had always been left open before, and that I needed my coat so I could walk home. He refused to open it, a job which would have required a minute of his time.

This was an impressive new low, even for Bill. I went to look for a teacher to appeal to, but by then everyone had left. I had no recourse; I ran home in a thin shirt and jeans, hair still wet from a shower, careening and sliding on patches of ice and snow.

When I walked in the door the first thing my puzzled parents wanted to know, of course, was where my coat was. Barely able to contain tears of rage, I told them what had happened.

My father got a look on his face I'd not seen before. He got up, grabbed the car keys, and said, "Get another coat on and come with me."

My mother was alarmed. "Stan, please don't do anything stupid."

Perhaps she felt a murder charge would harm my dad's reputation. I was willing to take that chance.

He did not say a word as we drove to the school. The door to the gym was still unlocked and we went in, but no one was there. We went into the hallway and I saw that the janitor's office was open, and we could hear noises coming from within. This was getting pee-in-your-pants exciting.

Wait, hold that pee. The janitor in the office was Gene, not Bill. Bill, it turned out, had gone home just a few minutes earlier. I can tell you now, without exaggeration, that this was one of the biggest disappointments in my life. I don't know about my father's.

Gene shook his head ruefully when I told him the story, and he readily opened the gate for me. I retrieved the coat, which had come so close to making my father and me town legends.

On the way home I asked my dad if he would have hit old asshole Bill. "I don't know," he replied, after a pause.

But I knew. If Bill had been there, one way or another he would have opened up that gate.

I don't have much respect for pacifists. There are people in this world who will run you into the ground unless you make a stand, and sometimes that requires more than calm and reasoned discourse. It may require at least the implied threat of violence, and in the rare instance, violence itself. Those whose top priority is to avoid trouble at any cost, to not get involved, are actually enablers of those who feel they are above the normal social conventions and constraints. By standing up for yourself, you stand up for the community of which you are a part.

If someone jumps ahead of you in the movie line, speak up. If your words fall on deaf ears, break something.

***

My mother, Eleanor, was a housewife in the days before that became disreputable. Her job was to cook and clean and spank Randy and me. All these things she did well. And often.

As skillful as she was in the kitchen, however, she lacked a flair for culinary adventure. Perhaps because my father was a no-nonsense meat-and-potatoes man, my mother had developed a rotating dinner menu that consisted of seven basic meals. Randy and I grew up on those seven meals: we hated four of them.

The worst one was beef tongue. It is extremely depressing to come home from a tough day at school to find a five-pound tongue draining in the sink, and even more so when you know that in a few hours you will be expected to eat that tongue, with a boiled-cabbage side.

That was another thing about my mother's meals—the side dishes never varied. Roasted chicken always came with scalloped potatoes and green beans, brisket with mashed potatoes and cooked carrots, steak with baked potatoes and peas.

Randy and I begged her for years to "make something different." Finally she broke down and spent the better part of an afternoon incarnating a recipe for Hawaiian chicken she had seen in *McCalls* magazine.

By suppertime an exotic aroma filled the house, driving Randy and me crazy with anticipation. After an interminable wait, we were summoned to the dinner table.

"What's this?" asked my father. Something in his tone implied that the verdict was already in. Everyone knew that chicken was supposed to come oven-roasted crispy, with scalloped potatoes and green beans. Yet here before us lay a chicken smothered in some kind of pineapple and raisin sauce, with rice on the side.

He took one bite of it, then silently got up from the table and poured himself a big bowl of Wheaties. No mere words could have been as devastatingly expressive as this cereal gambit.

Randy and I cleaned our plates and then made short work of my father's portion. We loved that meal.

My mother never made it again.

In addition to cooking, my mother was the designated spanker of the house. Before having kids, my parents were firm in their belief that physically punishing children was cruel and archaic. They were convinced (not having had them yet) that children were intelligent, sensitive beings who could be reasoned with, obviating the need for corporal corrections.

Randy and I set out immediately to disabuse them of this fantasy and were successful in short order. My mother did the rule-setting and the screaming, and my father the spanking. Normally our father's return from work at the end of the day was a happy time, but not when we knew he was bringing a spanking (prescribed by our mother) along with him.

I was seven when I staged a valiant revolt against parental tyranny. My assigned bedtime was eight o'clock, whether I was tired or not. This struck me as plain dumb and I really resented it. I'd always try to make myself very small on the couch while watching TV, in the hopes that I'd be overlooked. It never worked.

On the evening of my insurrection, a program was starting at eight that I badly wanted to watch. The calls for my retirement started coming a few minutes after. I, too, had a theory about parents: that they were, at heart, intelligent and sensitive beings who could be reasoned with. I tried this and was faced with a glaring counterexample to my hypothesis.

I had had seven years of being told what to wear, what to eat, when to eat, when to go out to play, when to come back in, when to go to bed, and I was fed up.

I politely declined my mother's invitation to go to bed. Then I politely refused her order to go to bed. That TV show was a must-see.

My father entered the negotiations: "Either you go to bed now, or I'm going to drag you in there."

"Go ahead," I said.

He got up and started pulling on my leg. I resisted.

He pulled me off the couch and started dragging me across the carpet. I resourcefully grabbed the leg of the coffee table as I went by and it started coming with us. I was very proud.

My father bent down and picked me up bodily, carried me into the bedroom, dropped me on the bed, and spanked my butt good. I thought this was a good time to drop the gladiator role, and I began to scream and cry for all I was worth and kept it up for minutes.

This was a good move on my part because my mother became concerned about the intensity and duration of my caterwauling, and wondered aloud whether my father had hit me a little too hard. Perhaps my dad wondered himself, because he declared that he would never hit my brother or me again. So my little rebellion had caused a rift within the ruling party, which was good. It was now up to my mother to do the dirty work. She was not as strong as my dad, so her handiwork was a bit low on power. Unfortunately, she realized this, too, so she made up for it by repetition.

I remember clearly the end of the spanking era. I was ten and I had committed another spank-worthy transgression of some sort or other. I was lying on my bed, with my rear in ready position. My mother wound up and let fly, but just before the blow hit home I rolled off the bed, abandoning it to its fate. Fate struck a millisecond later, actually raising a cloud of lint dust.

Randy and I thought this was about the funniest thing we had ever seen, and my mother fled both the room and the hysterical laughter that filled it. The spankings ended forever on that day, proving that discipline is no laughing matter.

***

Every Sunday morning my father prepared his own culinary specialty: pancakes. He used a big iron skillet and mixed several different types of flour together in some secret proportion. No one else could make pancakes that came close. Randy and I gorged on our syrup-laden pancakes while we watched the Lone Ranger outsmart the bad guys on TV. (The director of that show didn't know what he was doing. Every time the Lone Ranger said, "Now here's my plan, Tonto," a commercial would come on and we'd miss what the Lone Ranger said.)

Another ritual, the family drive, followed on Sunday afternoons, but this was one that Randy and I hated. We wanted to spend the afternoon playing with our friends, and then watch Marlin Perkins let hideous jungle creatures crawl all over him on *Zoo Parade*.

Instead, we were packed into the back seat of the Packard and spirited off into the countryside, where we always ended up at some creepy mansion or other where antiques were sold. What our parents saw in this dusty old crap completely escaped us, and we'd spend hours outside on the lawn or the porch, futilely trying to find something to do in the middle of nowhere. Worse, we just knew our friends back home had discovered buried treasure in the woods.

One Sunday we returned home to learn that Marlin Perkins had been bitten by a poisonous snake on live TV that very afternoon. The entertainment opportunity of a lifetime and we had missed it! We were mad at our parents for weeks. (Marlin lived.)

The end result of years of these Sunday drives was a house filled with antiques: chests, tables, chairs, figurines, etchings, and paintings. It was less than an ideal environment for two growing boys; "bulls in a china shop" quite literally sums it up.

The most prized piece in the whole house was an ornate lamp fashioned out of an alabaster vase rich in bas-relief. It sat on a table in the living room with all the gravity of a nuclear reactor. Whenever Randy or I moved any faster than a glacier through any part of the house someone would yell, "Be careful—you'll break the alabaster lamp!"

Breaking that lamp came to symbolize for us the absolute worst thing that a child could ever do. Like all well-adjusted kids, I had fleeting (sometimes lingering) fantasies of beating up my parents when they did something horrible, such as cutting off my allowance. But not even for a second did I ever contemplate doing in the alabaster lamp. It was simply unthinkable.

The lamp remained unharmed after ten years of beating the odds.

The lucky streak came to a skidding halt the day my father decided to show me the correct way to execute a hook shot. In the living room. As his fully-extended right arm swooped up in an elegant arc, his cupped fingers barely caught the underside of the lampshade. The shade flew off and the lamp went crashing toward the table. Exhibiting the reflexes of a guard, he managed to catch the lamp just as it made contact with the table, but a small alabaster chunk went dribbling across the table nevertheless.

Randy and I were transfixed. To actually see the lamp broken was like a horrible miracle, a religious man's vision of hell. My mother was furious. My father was mortified. He got some dental bonding material from his office and reattached the chunk. When the glue dried, the only clue to the accident was a fine line that betrayed the break. To this day I cannot look at the lamp without staring at that line and remembering its birth.

My hook shot did not improve.

***

Being the oldest child has always carried with it a high degree of status, especially if the child is male. This is an elaborate scam perpetuated by society to pacify the firstborn, because in reality they get screwed at every turn.

For parents the first child is a terrifying experiment from the day the rabbit calls in sick. The child is scrutinized mercilessly for things to brag about (he's only three months old and he absolutely demands the comic section with his breakfast), worry about (he seems to have no interest in computers at all), or both (did you see the way he was grabbing the baby sitter?).

Parents devour every book on child care ever written, and know to the day when a "normal" child says his first word, takes his first step, stops sucking his thumb, and wets his bed for the last time.

The first child is guarded relentlessly from the possibility of physical injury. He is not permitted to stand up on chairs, run

41

while holding anything sharper than a ball, climb trees higher than himself, or ride his bike beyond the driveway.

By the time the second child arrives the parents are so numb they barely look up as she hangs by the heels from her second-story bedroom window. She hasn't spoken a word by age eight because she's a late bloomer. And the fact that she disassembled the neighbors' cat with a hacksaw clearly indicates that she wants to be a veterinarian.

Randy reaped the second-child bonanza in full measure. When I was finally allowed to stay up until eight o'clock, so was he. My parents bought me my first bicycle when I was in the sixth grade. Randy got one at the same time—he was in the third grade. When my allowance was raised to fifty cents a week, so was Randy's, which meant that he was making twice as much money as I had at the same age. Even inflation couldn't account for that.

I don't remember consciously harboring any resentment toward Randy over any of this, but it may explain why one evening just before bath time I yielded to an irresistible impulse to piss all over him.

By some quirk of fate almost all of the kids in our immediate neighborhood were closer in age to me than to Randy. This meant that I usually had my little brother tagging along wherever I went. I could never allow myself to get totally caught up in the excitement of the moment because I was responsible for making sure Randy didn't get hurt.

This wasn't easy because Randy was always intent on proving himself worthy of our company. If we scaled a cliff that tested our limits and courage, Randy had to climb it, too. If we rocketed down a steep hill on our bikes, Randy did it without hands. If we threw snowballs at a neighbor's house, Randy aimed at the windows.

At times the job of protecting Randy from himself got too much for me. There was a very high telephone pole in our backyard which supported our TV antenna; spikes protruded from the sides of the pole to allow climbing for maintenance and repairs. Instead of measuring our progress in life with pencil marks on the wall charting our heights, my friends and I gauged our progress by how high up the pole we dared to climb. (Of course, climbing the pole was strictly forbidden to us.)

Randy always wanted to climb the pole, too, but he was too short to reach the first spike and so was quite literally grounded. He couldn't stand this, and he threw very impressive tantrums when I refused to hoist him up to get him started.

On one occasion he put on a particularly accomplished performance, and I couldn't stand it any more. I lifted him up and stood back just in time to see him slip and fall, knocking his front tooth loose on the way down. On the way back into the house, I tried to coach a bleeding and screaming Randy on an ingenious story about tripping and falling while playing tag. But when my distraught mother asked him what had happened, he caved immediately and sang like a bird in heat, knowing full well that he had the diplomatic immunity of being too young to know any better and I didn't. He was right, and for the next several days he had trouble chewing and I had trouble sitting.

I also had to protect Randy from the other kids. One afternoon he came home from school crying, a common occurrence. Usually it was because a teacher had punished him for absolutely no reason. But on this day he reported that a kid named Ricky had punched him in the face on the playground (for absolutely no reason).

The next day at school I cornered Ricky in the hallway, grabbed him by the shirt, and warned him that if he ever touched my brother again I would kill him. He punched me in the face and walked into the classroom rubbing his knuckles.

I had taught him not to mess with the Frieds.

Randy's personality was as different from mine as could be. I was analytical, studious, serious, and careful. Randy wasn't.

Nowhere were the differences between us more apparent than in the way we assembled model airplanes. I took all the pieces out of the box, carefully spread them out on the table, and matched up each one to the exploded diagram. I read the instructions from beginning to end, forming a mental image of how the plane was constructed. Only then did I allow myself to start slowly gluing pieces together.

Randy dumped his pieces on the floor, tossed the directions out of the way, and started gluing by dead reckoning. This gave Randy's work a signature look: his completed planes were always missing essential parts, ones he found out too late had to be inserted at an earlier stage. Often it was a wing.

This did not seem to bother him one bit.

As an adult, I have methodically worked myself through a series of safe, respectable, middle-class careers.

Randy is the multimillionaire founder of his own company, with a Hollywood-style house on a mountaintop overlooking the Hudson Valley.

***

My Uncle Dick always enjoyed teasing me. I used to wonder about the possible reason for this, and I finally concluded that either he liked me a lot or he didn't.

As a young man Dick had been in the Navy and was given the chance to become a naval pilot. It was a very tough decision for him, but ultimately he elected to leave the service in order to marry and start a career and family. But his desire to learn to fly never left him, and much later in life he fulfilled a dream and got his private pilot's license.

He invited me to go up with him. This put me into an emotional bind. I had been terrified the few times I had flown on a commercial jet, and I knew that small planes were much more dangerous. On the other hand, I knew it would be a thrill to see Catskill and the surrounding countryside from the air, and this might be the only opportunity I would have to do so.

The pros and cons were pretty evenly matched. The tiebreaker was the realization that if I declined the offer, no matter what excuse I came up with, Dick would have the raw material for a tease-fest that could well last the rest of my life.

I told him I'd love to.

It was a beautiful fall day in the Hudson Valley as I carefully watched Dick go through the preflight checks. He gave the air of knowing what he was doing, which was good.

Then we headed down the runway, gaining momentum, and I tried to keep calm by telling myself that, according to the laws of physics, once the plane reached a certain speed it *had* to take off.

And it did, but now I was really on edge because I knew that we were probably in the most risky portion of the whole flight. I listened intently to the engine noise for signs of trouble; I looked at Dick out of the corner of my eye to make sure he still seemed calm and in control. But despite my inner turmoil, I was sure that I was maintaining a relaxed demeanor for Dick. This was very important.

We were still ascending noisily when Dick spoke for the first time.

"Oh, shit!"

I was staring out the window when he said this, and it almost had the effect of a direct order. Not only was the comment ominous enough on its face, but it had been barely a week since I had read a chilling article in *Psychology Today* about the analysis of tape recordings in the cockpits of doomed airplanes. Curiously enough, in the majority of cases the pilots' last words were exactly the same:

"Oh, shit!"

I wanted to scream like a baby, but I knew I had to keep cool just in case we survived whatever was about to go down.

I waited a few seconds and then as casually as I could manage said, "What is it, Dick?"

"The air speed indicator. It's not working."

I waited another few seconds.

"Is that bad?"

"Well, you can fly without it, but it's better to have it."

We got up to 2,000 feet, leveled off, and began the tour. My heart, which was at 10,000 feet, also leveled off.

I calmed down enough to enjoy the sights, and then after thirty minutes we went back in and landed smoothly. I knew that I would never take being on the ground for granted again.

As we walked back from the plane, I said, "Dick, that was a lot of fun. Thanks for taking me up. But if you don't mind, I need to give you a little lesson in pilot etiquette. When you've got a passenger in your plane, and something minor goes wrong, especially on takeoff, do not say—I repeat—do not say, 'Oh, shit!'" And then I told him about the article.

I had never seen Dick laugh so hard as he did then, and I haven't seen him laugh as hard since. But he comes quite close every time he tells the story on me, which he continues to do at every family gathering.

I should have just saved myself the trouble and screamed like a baby when I had the chance—I wouldn't have come out of it any worse.

***

Grandparents rank high among a child's most valuable assets. They give you money for good report cards, buy you toys, and take you on exciting day trips. They never exact a price for any of this by spanking you.

My paternal grandmother, Pauline, died before I was old enough to form clear memories of her. Samuel, her husband, retired to Florida not long after, so I saw him only for a few days each year during our annual family vacation.

So it was left to my maternal grandparents, who lived in Catskill, to supply the bulk of my "grandma" and "grandpa" memories.

Jacob was Russian, and in 1914 his parents, fearing for his safety in the time of the pogroms, sent him to New York City on a steamer to live with an uncle. At fifteen years of age, with little money and no English, he came totally alone to this new world.

Upon arrival, one of the first things he noticed about Americans was that a lot of them seemed to be chewing something even when they weren't eating. Applying his own rural experience to this puzzle, he concluded that Americans chewed their cud. In time, he was immensely relieved to learn about chewing gum.

He worked hard to learn English and did well in school. He ultimately put himself through pharmacy school and married Manya, a Russian girl he met through relatives in New York.

They made their way to Catskill to purchase a drugstore, and over the years they had two daughters, Eleanor and Sybil. Eleanor had two sons, one of whom was me, and that's how I got to know Grandpa Jake.

Grandpa Jake was a character of mythic proportions.

As bitter as he was over Russia's treatment of the Jews, he never lost his love for the motherland. And he seemed to have taken some sort of a personal vow not to betray that love by absorbing any more of American culture than minimally necessary. He never lost his thick Russian accent, never picked up American slang. He resolutely refused to understand American humor.

Despite seventy years of living in America he never came close to comprehending American sports like baseball or football. Every October the same scene was replayed: the family would be sitting in the living room watching the World Series, and Jake would glance up from his newspaper.

"Why is that man running?"

"Because he just hit the ball and he's running to the base."

"So how come he stopped running?"

"Because the other team would have thrown him out at second base if he kept running."

"If he hits it over the fence can the other team get him out?"

"No, that's a home run, and he goes all the way around the bases and scores a run."

"So why didn't he hit it over the fence?"

"Because it's very hard to hit a home run."

"This is a dumb game." And he would make a big show of pulling the paper back up in front of his face so he couldn't see the dumb game any longer.

And every December we'd all be sitting in the living room watching the National Football League championship game.

"Why is that man running?"

"Because he's got the football and he's trying to run down the field to the other team's goal to score a touchdown."

"Why are they jumping on him like crazy people?"

"The other team is trying to prevent him from scoring by tackling him."

"But can't he get hurt?"

"Sometimes that happens."

"This is a dumb game." Up went the paper.

The only sport he seemed to understand was boxing, because there was no ball involved.

Every event in life reminded him of an "old Russian proverb." These proverbs usually involved animals and were totally lacking in either sense or relevance. I might break a toy and be crying over it, and he would say something like, "There's an old Russian proverb about times like this. The pig that you name today you find in your soup tomorrow." These proverbs often made us cry even harder.

***

Grandpa Jake obtained his driver's license long before the advent of driving tests. This was the only way he could possibly have gotten one, because he was the worst driver imaginable.

The only rule of the road he seemed to recognize was that you should stop for a red light. Other than that, he just used his common sense. This was not a big help.

One night our whole family was going out for pizza, my father at the wheel. We came upon a slower car in front of us.

"Pass him now," said Grandpa Jake.

"I can't," said my father. "It's a double white line."

"So what?" asked Grandpa Jake.

"Do you know what a double white line means?" asked my father.

"Sure," said Grandpa Jake, sounding insulted. "It means you should be doubly careful when you pass."

At the time of this incident my grandfather had been terrorizing the roads for fifty years.

Not only did he know nothing about the rules of the road, he observed only what lay dead ahead (or, perhaps more accurately, what was about to be dead ahead). Anything else was irrelevant.

Grandpa Jake cut people off with impunity, passed cars and then slowed down, pulled out in front of speeding vehicles, wandered into other lanes at random, and scattered pedestrians at crosswalks. He was never aware of any of it. This is even worse than doing such things on purpose, for in that case, at least, it might be possible to reform.

On one occasion we watched Grandpa Jake retrieve his car from a supermarket parking lot. He hit a total of three cars while pulling out of his parking space. He was aiming for the fourth when I, running frantically, reached his car and banged on his window. He huffily denied everything, not believing that an expert driver could hit another car without knowing it.

For Grandpa Jake, defensive driving meant scaring everyone else on the road so badly that they wouldn't dare get close enough to let him do any harm.

And since he thought so highly of his driving ability, he felt obligated to impart his skills to Randy and me—even though we were only seven and ten at the time. So every weekend he would take us to an empty parking lot and let us drive around. He would sit in the front seat and read the paper, obviously very proud of the fact that he had taught two small children to drive in so short a time.

One evening Randy and I walked up to Grandpa Jake's because he had promised to take us to a movie. He was running late in finishing his dinner, so to save time he gave us the keys and told us to pull the car out of the garage.

We were thrilled and proud to be entrusted with this adult chore, but as soon as we got out to the garage the inevitable fight started. Who was going to drive? We argued about who was the better driver until Randy finally resorted to his ace-in-the-hole negotiating tactic of simulating a hydrophobic fit.

So Randy got behind the wheel, and I stood in the driveway to guide him out of the garage. He put the car in reverse and then carefully and skillfully backed the car out of the narrow doorway opening, while I checked for adequate clearance on each side.

We came very close to making it. As the front of the car cleared the doorway, the flared bumper hooked the wooden doorjamb. Randy kept right on coming, and so did a substantial portion of the garage.

We argued about whose fault it was, but it was a tough call. We started crying in unison and went in to tell Grandpa Jake that we had pulled the car and part of the garage out of the garage.

He went out to look and it was as if he couldn't believe his eyes. How could two people whom he had taught to drive do such a thing?

"Go home," he said gruffly. "We're not going to the movies."

We walked home, thoroughly dejected at having let Grandpa Jake down, and we had little choice but to tell our mother why we were home so early. As expected, she got terribly angry, but to our immense relief it was directed at Grandpa Jake, instead of us.

She tried to call him to chew him out, but there was no answer. Just then the front doorbell rang. I ran to the door and opened it and there was Grandpa Jake at the bottom of the hall.

"Come on, we're going to be late."

"But I thought we weren't going anymore."

"Do you want to go or don't you?"

I ran and got Randy, and we hightailed it out of there before my mom had a chance to collar Grandpa Jake.

Eventually the garage got fixed, but the driving lessons stopped. Apparently Grandpa Jake had concluded that we were unteachable.

***

Grandpa Jake was an inveterate tinkerer. He had a workbench in his cellar, with tools of all descriptions strewn about in total disorder. He would never buy anything that he could make, even if what he made didn't work.

One summer he fashioned a wheelbarrow for his garden out of scrap lumber. The handles were two-by-fours, with the ends whittled down so you could grip them. Instead of one wheel in the front he had two, on the theory that it would be twice as easy to maneuver. He was extremely proud of his creation and couldn't wait to show everyone. My father attempted to pick it up and push it, but it was so heavy he almost herniated himself.

"You picked it up too fast," Grandpa Jake insisted.

He persisted in using it for several weeks. We knew this because we could trace his comings and goings by the three-inch-deep muddy ruts in the lawn.

One day we went to visit him and found a store-bought wheelbarrow in the garage, and no sign of the Frankenbarrow. We asked him what had happened to it.

"Somebody stole it."

This was the paradigm Grandpa Jake explanation. It allowed him to save face while replacing the monstrosity with a wheelbarrow that worked, and more than this, it declared to the world that someone else out there had coveted the contraption enough to swipe it.

***

Grandma Manya was a simple, kind woman whose main priority in life was to prevent Randy and me from catching a cold. This was a full-time job because, in Grandma's medical opinion, almost anything that did not involve sleeping or eating could cause a cold. Going outside without a coat in any season, playing too hard, getting overheated, handling snow with bare hands, staying up too late—all such activities were dangerous invitations to viral predators.

Of course, Randy and I would make a big show of doing exactly the thing she was warning against, and she would go off in a state of incredulity to complain to our mother that she wasn't raising us right. We loved that.

Manya didn't call Grandpa "Jake" like everyone else did. She referred to him as "the Crazy One." Any time you talked to Grandma the first thing she would tell you was what the Crazy One had done on that particular day. Like the time it was pouring rain and Grandpa Jake had no umbrella in the drugstore. Needing to run an errand, he grabbed an empty cardboard shipping box that said "KOTEX" on all four sides, poked two eyeholes out of it, and ambled down Main Street with it over his head.

When he tried to cross the street, the local cop on the beat stopped him and made him take off the box, just to see who the damned fool was. When he saw it was Jake, he put the box back over him and told him to look both ways.

Manya and Grandpa Jake were constantly at war over the thermostat in their house. She liked it warm and kept turning the heat up; he liked it cool and kept turning the heat down.

One winter day a strange thing happened. After Jake left for the drugstore, Manya started feeling too hot in the house. She attempted to turn the thermostat down (a totally novel experience for her) but found that she couldn't budge the control lever. As the morning progressed she got hotter and hotter, but still she couldn't adjust the thermostat.

Finally, on the verge of passing out, she called the Crazy One at the store and told him the thermostat was reading ninety degrees. He didn't believe this for a second. He told her to leave the thermostat alone, that everything was fine. Then he hung up on her.

A short time later Manya called again and said that the thermostat was pointing to ninety-five and it sounded like the boiler in the cellar was going to blow up.

The Crazy One said that there was nothing wrong, that he had "fixed" the thermostat once and for all and that she was to leave it alone. Then he hung up on her. Again.

But Grandpa Jake began to think about it, and a wispy cloud of doubt began to drift over his horizon. He had indeed fixed the thermostat. In a brilliant maneuver to end the tug-of-war once and for all, he had drilled a small hole through the control lever and screwed it in position at seventy degrees. Now nobody could move it without the aid of a small screwdriver.

So why was Manya acting so frantic? She of all people was complaining that it was unbearably hot inside; at seventy degrees she would normally be entering the late stages of frostbite. This did not make sense. After fretting for a time he finally decided to go home and check.

When he entered the house it was approaching 100 degrees inside and the boiler was roaring like a freight train. He ran for the screwdriver, removed the screw, and pushed the control down to zero. But the boiler wouldn't stop.

In a panic, he called the heating contractor, who rushed right over (this was a small town, remember, and a long time ago).

After a brief inspection the repairman asked, "Jake, you trying to blow up the house?"

When Grandpa Jake drilled the hole in the control lever, tiny metal shavings had fallen down into the thermostat and created a short-circuit. From then on, as far as the boiler was concerned, it was damn the torpedoes and full steam ahead.

The thermostat was replaced, Jake paid a hefty bill, and Manya had her Crazy One story for the day.

***

Grandpa Jake had a psychotic hatred of rats. I knew nothing of this until the day I found out firsthand.

Grandpa Jake sold ice cream and candy bars in his drugstore on Main Street, and Randy and I were each allowed one treat a day. On this particular summer afternoon a marching band competition was kicking off with a procession down Main Street, and I decided I needed a candy bar to enhance the parade experience.

As I opened the door to the drugstore, a gigantic sewer rat that had been rousted from its quarters by all the noise ran right through my legs and into the store.

Grandpa Jake was waiting on a customer at the front counter. He saw me opening the door to let in what he took to be my own personal rat, and he went ballistic.

"What did you let that rat in here for?" he kept screaming.

He ran into the back room and emerged with a pistol. The rat did not take this as a good sign and scurried down one of the aisles. Grandpa Jake chased after it, firing away and calling the rat very bad names.

The first two shots took out some bottled merchandise. The third shot took out the rat. I was still standing in the middle of the store, deafened by the noise, totally astounded at what I was witnessing and wondering if I was next. The customer was still standing at the counter, probably contemplating my grandfather's advertising slogan, *Your Friendly Neighborhood Drugstore*.

I ran out of there without my candy bar and didn't stop until I got home. Now any normal parent upon hearing such a story from an excited child would have the good sense to dismiss it out of hand. But this was Grandpa Jake. My mother didn't doubt it for an instant.

She called him up and a heated argument ensued.

"Dad, he did *not* let the rat in on purpose."

"It was *not* his rat."

"How can you shoot a gun with a child standing there?"

"What do you mean he wasn't near the rat? Does a bullet know from near?"

From that time on I never entered the store without checking to see if I was being tailed. And, of course, from then on I always wanted Grandpa Jake to show me his gun. He always proudly obliged.

***

Perhaps my most enduring memory of Grandpa Jake is the time he rescued me from the depths of childhood despair. In those days I got an allowance of a quarter a week. I was very good at saving my money, and after a few months I had managed to save a dollar. It was an exciting milestone to be able to trade in those four pieces of metal for a crisp bill, and I treasured it.

I wandered around toy stores with that bill in my pocket, looking at all the things I could buy. But I never found anything worth trading that bill for.

One day Grandpa Jake was driving to Albany and invited me to go along. He said we could visit a large toy store, and surely I would find something to buy there. He was wrong. There were certainly many more toys than I was used to seeing in the small stores in Catskill. But I walked out of that store, too, with the bill clutched tightly in my pocket. I wasn't going to part with it until I had found the perfect toy.

Sitting in the back seat on the way home, I pulled out a piece of gum, popped it in my mouth, and stuck the wrappers in my pocket. But I didn't like the way they felt there, so after a while I reached in, grabbed them, and tossed them out the window.

A few minutes later it was time to look at my dollar again, on the off chance that it had changed into a five. I reached into my now empty pocket, and as my fingers bottomed out my heart froze in my chest. It couldn't be! It was too horrible to be possible.

I searched the back seat like a madman, crying uncontrollably. I was still crying when we reached home. My parents happened to be standing in the yard when we arrived, and I bolted out of the car and grabbed on to my mother's leg, trying to explain through my sobs what had happened.

Before I got very far, Grandpa Jake called to me: "Hey, Denny, look." He was turned around, gazing toward the back seat. I went to the car and peered through the window. A crumpled up dollar bill lay stuck in the crevice at the back of the seat.

"You didn't throw it out after all. It must have fallen out of your pocket when you grabbed the wrappers and gotten stuck back there."

My relief and happiness were boundless. Never again in my entire life have I experienced such a complete and sudden reversal of fortune (in the good direction, that is). I couldn't understand how it had happened, because on the way home I had searched every inch of that back seat in the desperate hope that some such fluke had occurred. I felt like one of the luckiest people alive.

It wasn't until many years later that, as I was recalling the incident, the truth flashed like lightning.

I had been lucky.

4

The Neighborhood

Our own backyard was one of the most active and significant battlegrounds in world history. When the proper authorities finally recognize this fact, I expect the blue plaque to read as follows:

> ON THIS SITE, THROUGHOUT THE 1950S, THOUSANDS OF BATTLES WERE FOUGHT BETWEEN COWBOYS AND INDIANS, KNIGHTS AND DRAGONS, COPS AND ROBBERS, GLADIATORS AND PEASANTS, JUNGLE EXPLORERS AND NATIVES, YANKS AND JAPS, YANKS AND KRAUTS, AND SPACE CADETS AND ALIENS.

The combatants in any particular battle depended on the last Saturday matinee we had seen; and rarely did we miss a Saturday matinee. Like metal shavings drawn to a magnet, kids from all parts of town converged on the Community Theater to spend the afternoon cheering our heroes, eating popcorn, throwing candy, spying on couples necking in the last row, sneaking a smoke, and kicking the seat in front of us.

Those were the days when theaters were serious about giving customers their money's worth, which for us kids was all of fifteen cents. First there was the Movietone newsreel, then a cartoon followed by the coming attractions, and then a double feature. When we finally left the theater, the bright world outside was like a shocking new discovery.

Besides the pure entertainment value, the movies taught us valuable survival skills. For instance, if you step in quicksand, instead of scrambling frantically to get out like the bad guys always did (their jungle hats were the last thing you saw), you just gently roll out, like Tarzan always did. We roamed the neighborhood looking for quicksand so we could practice, but mud puddles were the best we could do.

If you're ever in a burning plane, confidently kick open the door and jump out. Then start looking for the parachute that is almost certainly falling down beside you among the debris. Put it on and pull the cord—the chute will open seconds before you hit the ground and will get hung up in a tree. Get your knife out and cut the lines, and drop into the large haystack that will be directly below you. Then look for the beautiful country girl who has been mute since childhood and take it from there.

And if you encounter a malevolent, superpowerful robot bent on destruction, just ask it a paradoxical riddle such as "Have you stopped beating your robot wife yet?" You'll fry its electronic brain. Smoke will actually come out of its head.

Yet my fondest memory of those Saturday matinees has nothing to do with the images on the screen. It involves the balcony candy machine and the joys of petty theft.

The candy machine had an art deco look and was built like a safe. We put our nickel in the slot, decided which type of candy we wanted, pulled the appropriate lever all the way out and then released it so it would snap back into place. One box of candy would come down the chute. Before we left we also banged on the coin return a few times and savagely kicked the machine in the hope of loosening some change. But this was merely ritualistic behavior and never worked.

Then one day a Big Kid (more about them later) showed us something miraculous. Instead of releasing the lever so that it snapped back into place, he oh-so-slowly and carefully eased it in until he heard a faint click and then he pulled it back out again. Down came his box of candy—and he still had control of the lever! He repeated the maneuver and another box of candy fell. And then another and another, until his nerves finally got to him and he eased the lever in too far and it locked back into place. But he had earned five boxes of candy for his nickel, as well as the awe of us spectators. He sauntered off with his head tilted back, guzzling an entire box of candy at once.

I cannot begin to describe to you the impact this spectacle had on our young lives. It completely dominated our thoughts and made concentrating in school just about impossible. Over the next few matinees we too began to develop the technique. It required the touch of a safecracker and nerves of steel, especially when we put our only nickel in the slot. Most of the time we managed to get two or three boxes. The record was six. But woe to the clumsy fool who tightened up at the crucial moment and managed to get only one box of candy for his nickel, for not only would he be subjected to a full week of scorn and derision, he also had to nurse his snack piece by piece while his cronies drained their booty a box at a shot.

Beating that machine became the whole point of going to the movies. I dreamed about it at night, an endless series of perfect moves, boxes of candy piling up around me.

We knew it couldn't last. Sooner or later, we feared, the candyman had to notice the machine's wide disparity between output and income and track down the problem. Every Saturday as we made our highly anticipated march toward the scene of the (hoped for) crime, we were on edge, wondering if our *candy ex-machina* had been relegated to the realm of legend. And week after week our fears proved groundless, as our touch became more refined and the harvest more bountiful.

Then finally that terrible day: the lever felt different right away, tighter, without play, in control. First one of us failed, then another, and another. We couldn't all be having a bad day at the same time. There was only one conclusion: it was over.

We moped back to our seats, the spring gone from our steps. And there we sat for the rest of the afternoon, each of us slowly nibbling his one bought-and-paid-for box of candy, a piece at a time. Going to the Saturday matinee never again felt the same.

The candy dreams continued for some time until, as I got older, they transformed into the adult version. I would be walking across a lawn and suddenly spot a dollar bill lying there. I'd pick it up and then spy another. And then two. More over there. And there's a bill half buried. Pull it out, start digging. More.

You get the idea. But, unlike the candy dream, the money dream never got played out in reality. Only one time in my life have I found a bill on the ground. I had just parked my car in front of the apartment complex where I lived, and when I got out I saw a dollar bill on the grass near the base of a tree. I snatched it up and my pulse rate doubled. Surely more bills were scattered about, just like in the dream. I walked slowly around and around that tree in ever widening circles. I looked up in the tree. Beat some bushes. Kicked some dirt around. Zilch.

If any of my neighbors had seen me, surely they called the local psychiatric hospital to inquire about escapees. They couldn't possibly know that they were only witnessing one man's heroic efforts to make his dreams come true.

***

When I was growing up all our immediate neighbors were insane people.

On one side of us were the Coopers, an elderly couple who periodically came out of their house to throw half-eaten fruit over the wooden fence into our yard. Or to snatch up any ball that we had the misfortune to let bounce over the fence.

One time Mr. Cooper was standing in front of his house on Main Street, and as my seventy-five-year-old Grandpa Jake passed by, Mr. Cooper cursed at him. Grandpa Jake decked him with one punch and was promptly arrested for assault. We were as proud of him as could be.

On the other side of us lived the widow Mrs. Wilson, whose husband had understandably committed suicide years before. Mrs. Wilson chased us with a broom if we played too close to her house, and one time she tried to pour water on us from her second-story window. Her aim was bad and she succeeded only in terrifying her pet cat.

The Rivers, an elderly mother-and-daughter team, lived directly across the street from us; their sole mission in life was to catch one of us on their lawn. This made their yard the prime piece of playground real estate in the area; kids would trek from distant neighborhoods just to stampede over it.

One day a neatly printed sign on a wooden post appeared in the middle of the lawn: PLEASE KEEP OFF THE GRASS, it implored. Somehow the Rivers must have felt that the power of the written word would have an effect that their verbal threats lacked. It did. Within ten minutes one of us (unidentified even to this day) had thrown a brick, shattering the sign and the post all in one shot.

Next to the Rivers lived the Walkers, another elderly couple who not only guarded their lawn but also the public sidewalk in front of their house. Randy and I were on the way home from school one afternoon and we made the mistake of walking on "their" sidewalk. (Okay, it's possible that we also accidentally threw a chestnut at their house on the way by.) Mrs. Walker popped out of her front door like a cuckoo clock and started shrieking.

I leaned over and whispered in Randy's ear, "She's a damn son-of-a-bitch."

Randy must have agreed with me because he promptly yelled out, "Yeah, you're a damn sonamabitch."

By the time we got home, the call had already been made and our mother was waiting. I stood accused of telling Randy (who, of course, was too young to know any better) to call Mrs. Walker "a son-of-a-bitch." I attempted to defend myself, but my mother couldn't seem to grasp my distinction between reporting a fact and issuing an order. This failure on her part cost me two weeks' allowance.

Over the years our parents continually admonished us not to antagonize the neighbors. But that would have left us with little reason to live.

***

My best friend was either Andy, Teddy, or John. This varied on a daily basis, depending on whom I had played with most recently and whether or not it had ended in a fight.

Andy lived a few houses up the street. His parents had both come from Italy and spoke English with thick accents that were hard for us kids to decipher. His father, Sam, was the caretaker at a nearby Catholic monastery, and he built marvelous things with wood, including the family's large two-story house.

Sam usually didn't have much to say, but there were times, most often on lazy summer afternoons, when he would sit in the rocker on the back porch and tell us stories about the old country. We couldn't understand anything he said, but we knew it must be funny because he would laugh as he talked, so we laughed, too.

Andy's mother, Natalie, was a good, sweet lady who kept an immaculate house and raised two older children in addition to Andy. Natalie was the patron saint of the spaghetti sauce that simmered eternally on the kitchen stove, filling the house with an aroma that always made Randy and me wish we could put ourselves up for adoption.

Andy gave me my first lesson on the power of religion. My parents were ethnically Jewish, but the sum total of my religious education was a 3-D comic book based on the Old Testament. I loved that book, especially the story about Samson, but I couldn't figure out why they had omitted the chapters on Superman and Batman. (As a result of my parents' philosophy of letting children make up their own minds about religious matters, my only conscious connection as an adult with being Jewish is the occasional irresistible urge to lend money at high rates.)

On a sunny spring afternoon Andy and I set out on one of our typical bike adventures. We pedalled a few miles out of town into the countryside, just far enough so that we were intoxicated by the feeling of being completely on our own, in a place we had reached totally under our own power. And who could really know what insane axe murderer or insomniac mummy might just be lurking nearby?

We deposited our bikes in tall grass and found a shady spot under a tree, where we began to devour the Power Bars we had packed as rations. But on this particular day things did not proceed normally. Andy was halfway through his candy bar when he suddenly jumped up holding his throat, spitting out gobs of wet chocolate and screaming.

I was scared to death, but try as he might Andy couldn't mouth the words to tell me what was wrong. Was he choking on the candy bar? Had he just caught a glimpse of Godzilla through the treetops?

Finally, through his sobs, I made out what he was saying.

"I'm gonna die. I'm gonna die. I'm gonna die."

This was not good news.

"Why, Andy? What's the matter? Please tell me!" I stole a glance at the treetops. Nothing out of the ordinary. "Andy, please, what's the matter?"

"The candy bar! I'm gonna die! God's gonna kill me!"

Now we were getting somewhere. Nobody in my Bible comic had been struck down for eating a Power Bar, but maybe Andy had a more recent issue.

"Why is God gonna kill you?"

"Lent! I gave up candy for Lent! I forgot! I'm gonna die!"

I had never heard of Lent, but it was obvious that it had something to do with God and candy. And I knew that Andy was in need of some serious ministering.

So I, the little agnostic, explained to Andy how God was good and kind, and how He punished only people who did bad things on purpose. And since God knew everything, He knew that Andy didn't do this terrible thing on purpose. He would forgive Andy and not kill him.

"Do you really think so? Honest to God?"

"Honest to God."

He stopped crying and slowly calmed down. I had never in my life seen someone so afraid, and it had a lasting effect on me. Still, I would have taken advantage of the situation and eaten the rest of his Power Bar, but it was covered with spit.

That incident aside, Andy was fun to play with because he always supplied the background music to our adventures. Whether we were exploring the African jungle or blowing away invaders from space with atomic pistols, Andy always hummed an appropriate tune. He didn't even realize he was doing it, but hundreds of hours of Saturday double features had left his subconscious with the certain knowledge that absolutely nothing exciting happens in life without background music.

Andy's favorite TV show was *Highway Patrol*, with Broderick Crawford, and he never missed it. This was the source of a problem, however. The show was on from 1:00 to 1:30 Saturday afternoons, and the movie matinee started at 1:15. At about 1:28 Andy would come bounding down the concrete stairs in our backyard, humming an especially urgent tune, and we'd scramble down Main Street to the theater. By the time we bought our popcorn and soda and found our seats, we'd have missed the newsreel and, if our luck was running especially bad, part of the cartoon.

Missing the newsreel didn't bother us because it was virtually the same every week: battleships steaming somewhere on the high seas, Ike playing golf, and bespectacled, nerdy scientists in white coats peering at stuff in a test tube that promised to solve all the world's problems by the end of the week.

Missing the cartoon was another story.

Andy, unlike the rest of us, remained true to his childhood fantasy and grew up to become a policeman. I'm sure that he hums when he arrests people.

***

Teddy lived next to Andy and was the oldest of what eventually turned out to be seven kids. His father was a good-hearted but stern Irishman, about 4'10" tall and creatively nicknamed Shorty. Teddy's mother was Italian and permanently joined at the hip to a baby.

Teddy was the only friend of mine who went to the Catholic school in town, St. Patrick's Academy, and it was because of him that I developed a real fear of priests and nuns, even though they had no connection at all with my world.

From Teddy I learned that the nun teachers would make you lay your hands flat on the desk and then pummel your knuckles with a wooden ruler. They'd hold a paper bag over your head until you either cried or almost passed out, and then describe in excruciating detail how you would burn in hell forever. And if you really screwed up, you were then sent to a priest for the final judgment.

The nuns lived in a house next to the church. Every kid avoided that house as if it were haunted, the yard and sidewalk included. We would dare one another to sneak up on the porch and ring the doorbell, but no one ever accepted the challenge. What if you weren't quick enough, and a black-robed arm shot out of the door and grabbed you and pulled you in and they all descended on you like frenzied buzzards and clawed the flesh from your bones? It could happen. I mean, if they tortured kids like that in school, imagine what they could do if they got one alone in their house!

Teddy solved a few mysteries for me and introduced a few new ones. For example, for as long as I could remember I had noticed people with a very strange tic. For no apparent reason,

and at the oddest times, they would suddenly touch their fore-
heads and then their chests and then their shoulders in an odd
pattern. I saw a kid swimming once and his affliction seemed to
overcome him every time he prepared to go underwater. I saw
other kids doing it before they came to bat in a baseball game.

I tried it myself a few times just to see what it felt like. It
was complicated. I could understand an unconscious twitch of
the lip, or a quick bite on your thumbnail. But this other thing—
how could someone not know he was doing it?

Then one day I saw that poor Teddy had also become af-
flicted, and I got up enough courage to ask him about it. He told
me it was a religious gesture called "crossing yourself." So one
of the great mysteries of my childhood was solved: all of those
people who I thought suffered a serious disability were, in fact,
just praying.

One day after school Teddy had to run an errand to the
church, and I went with him. This was the first time I had ever
entered a church, and I felt like a great explorer. As we entered
the vestibule, Teddy went over to what looked like a birdbath,
dipped the fingers of his right hand into it and then crossed himself. Now we had another mystery.

On the way home I asked him, "What's the deal with the
water?"

"It's holy water," he explained.

To me it had looked like ordinary water. "Why is it holy?"

"Because the priest blessed it."

"Well, where does it come from?"

I expected him to say something like "an eternal spring in
Jerusalem where Jesus stopped once to take a drink."

"From the tap in the church kitchen."

So once again I was faced with the kind of puzzle that children wrestle with for years, where they understand the words
that are being used to explain something, but the concept itself
remains out of reach.

Could any tap water become holy water? What if it was polluted? If you drank holy water would you turn into Superman? If you had a gallon of holy water and mixed in a gallon of ordinary water, would you then have two gallons of holy water or two gallons of nonholy water?

For some reason Teddy had never asked himself these questions. It was just holy water, that's all. Why worry about it?

Teddy's uncritical acceptance of holy water (and Andy's of Lent) was representative of a phenomenon which puzzled me more the older I got. As we kids learned more about how the world worked, learned how to measure our opinions and beliefs against the yardstick of accumulated human knowledge and evidence, our fairy tales were slowly stripped away like layers of an onion. The Easter bunny went. Bye-bye tooth fairy. It was nice believing in you, Santa Claus.

But there seemed to be one fairy tale that even adults were expected to hang on to. A fifteen-year-old who leaves cookies and milk by the fireplace on Christmas Eve would be considered a prime candidate for psychological counseling. An adult who drops to his knees in an empty room and cries aloud for help in resisting the devil would be considered a religious man (and a probable shoo-in for political office).

Growing up, I spent a significant amount of time trying to figure out the difference between the two cases.

***

Three other mysteries haunted me in those early years.

The first was, how could a ship leave New York, head out over an ocean that looked exactly the same in all directions, and arrive exactly at its destination, say Lisbon? I could understand how someone got from point A to point B in a car, since there was a road with signs to follow. But in the ocean there were no roads and no signs. My father said it was done by radio, but I couldn't understand how listening to Perry Como singing "Hot Diggedy Dog" could help in getting to Lisbon.

The next puzzle was trying to figure out what was meant by a foreign language. A chair was a chair. A table was a table. Things were what they were, and who cared where someone was brought up? How could there be any language other than English, which identified exactly what things were?

Of course, I knew that people could play games and agree among themselves, for instance, that when someone said "hotongas" they meant "titties." But this in no way shed any light on the notion of a different language because everyone would know that when one of them said "hotongas" it was just code for "titties." There was just no way around them. "Titties" was titties.

And finally, I could not comprehend why people let themselves die. I understood getting crushed to death by Godzilla or being obliterated by a space weapon—nothing to be done there. But how could someone be sitting in a chair or lying in a bed and just let go?

My parents had told me that dying was kind of like going to sleep. This didn't help because no matter how tired I was, I could always make myself stay awake a little longer. I did it all the time when I was watching television. And that was just for a lousy TV show. How much more incentive would there be if letting go was forever?

Forget about it! If you feel that you're about to die, get up, take a quick walk around the block, drink a milkshake, go to the movies. Just keep putting it off. Why hadn't people figured this out?

So there you have my four greatest childhood mysteries: holy water, ships crossing the ocean, foreign languages, and death.

Forty years later I still don't understand three of them. (I've since learned a little Spanish.)

***

John was my third best friend. He excelled in any sport he tried. Of all the neighborhood kids, he was the fastest swimmer and runner, the best baseball and basketball player. No one dared pick a fight with him, either.

People who are good at everything are often insufferable egotists. But not John. He just did what he did and never seemed to notice how good he was at doing it. He could beat you at a game twenty times in a row and be just as happy to play you the twenty-first time, simply for the pure joy of playing.

A funny thing about people from your past—you may have known them for half a lifetime, yet your defining images of them often boil down to a few crystalline moments. And so it is that I'll always remember John limping hurriedly down a sidewalk.

He had suffered a badly sprained ankle a few days before and was getting around on crutches. But John couldn't stand to be a mere spectator at the neighborhood softball game that evening, so it was arranged that he would be a designated hitter for both teams, and that someone would run for him whenever he hit the ball.

Midway through the game, John hobbled up to the plate, threw his crutches to the side, and then proceeded to hit the ball farther than anyone I had ever seen before on that field. It went over center field, over the street, across a lawn and a porch, and directly through the second-story window of a house owned by a crotchety old coot who was constantly calling the police even when we hadn't done anything.

This time we had done something.

We all ran like hell—except for John, who was left standing on the completely empty softball field, a bat in his hands and a pair of crutches at his side. I had run down the block before I even dared look around, and that's when I saw him gimping frantically down the sidewalk, still holding the bat. His crutches were nowhere to be seen, and neither were any of his friends.

And that's the picture I will always carry of John.

At an early age I learned a universal truth about friends—no matter who your friends are, or how many they number, they will never all like one another at the same time. Alliances shift, mutual interests wax and wane, subtle jealousies reach critical mass and erupt. And you're left in the middle, trying to keep it all straight so you don't commit the social faux pas of including two enemies in the same activity. Of course, the party you leave out in the interest of social stability will then hate you for the omission.

Most of the time in our neighborhood expediency won out. We might not like Joe, but if he was the only one around that had a football or basketball, Joe would get the call. If another ball became available, Joe could blow it out his ass.

And so another useful lesson in life was revealed: It's not what you know or whom you know—it's having the balls at the right time.

***

Not everything in Catskill was named after Rip Van Winkle. The elementary school in my neighborhood was the Washington Irving School, named after the creator of Rip Van Winkle.

When we were not in school we could usually be found on the school playground, which had everything: swings of various types and sizes, monkey bars, slides, a basketball court, a sandlot baseball field, and a long, steep hill that was perfect for winter sledding.

It also had what we feared most in life: Big Kids. Big Kids preyed on us like lions after gazelle. And like the gazelle, our main protection was the anonymity afforded by staying in groups. But if we were careless enough to get caught walking home alone, or if we were so involved in the excitement of a game that we heedlessly chased a ball into their midst, we were dead meat.

Big Kid threats tended to be seasonal. During the winter we feared the torture known as "the Refrigerator Box Express." An appliance store on Main Street often put out empty cardboard refrigerator boxes for the garbage pickup. During the winter these boxes were valued commodities because, when taken to the playground and dragged up the hill, they became enclosed sleds that could be shared by several friends at once. We'd set the box at the crest of the hill, aim it down the middle, clamber in and rock forward a few times, and down we went, bouncing and flying and skimming, laughing all the way down with the pure, childhood, scary thrill of it all.

This was repeated until either the box broke down, or the Big Kids overcame their cold-weather inertia and issued the feared command: "All you little kids, over here." We had no choice but to obey. Escape might be possible, but then they would owe you one. Better to just get it over with.

They would stuff us all into the box. If there were enough of us, we ended up sitting on one another for lack of space. Then they would close the box up tight and shove it down the hill. This, then, was the infamous Refrigerator Box Express.

If the Big Kids were in a benevolent mood they shoved the box straight down the hill. We would jostle around inside like tightly packed marbles, but at least the ride was predictable.

Most of the time, though, they shoved the box down the hill sideways. This resulted in the box cartwheeling over and over on the way down, kids tumbling around inside like hamsters caught inside a wheel and sometimes spewing out like colorful cannonballs if the box broke open.

After such a ride the more delicate among us would set out for home, crying all the way. The others would go marching back up the hill again, and by their very presence dare the Big Kids to try it again. Which, of course, they did.

But there was a special time when it was relatively safe to be near the Big Kids: when they settled down under the apple tree next to the ball field to smoke and tell dirty jokes. The Big Kids didn't mind us then because we provided them with an extremely attentive audience. In return we learned about farmers' daughters and traveling salesmen. And we increased our vocabularies.

We often didn't know just what these new words meant. We just knew that the Big Kids were using them and that they sounded extremely cool.

One evening, after a particularly enlightening afternoon listening to the Big Kids, Randy and I were seated at dinner with my mother and father.

Randy: "Pass the fuckin' butter."

Me: "Here, you fucker. Give me that fuckin' bread."

Randy: "Fuck you, that's mine."

Our parents continued eating without showing the slightest sign of distress, obviously testing the theory that if outrageous behavior in children is ignored, they'll soon go on to something else.

Me: "Did you see that big fuckin' dog on the playground this afternoon?"

Randy: "Fuck, yeah, I saw him."

Me: "Who the fuck did it belong to?"

Randy: "Fuck me if I know."

By now my mother had stopped eating and was staring hard at my father. He cleared his throat and, as casually as he could, said, "You know, you've got to be careful with that word. A lot of people would be very offended if they heard you say it. So please don't say it anymore."

At that moment we realized that the Big Kids had introduced us to a whole new wonderful world of offensive language. And for the first time we began to view the Big Kids as possible allies rather than enemies.

In fact, I actually had two friends who were Big Kids, Tommy and Irwin. They lived only a few doors down the street from us and I had grown up with them, although they each had a three-year head start.

Their families were far from well-to-do, but every Christmas each one of them got an entire toy store of his own (which might explain why their families were far from well-to-do).

On Christmas mornings, after Randy and I each opened our two presents, one of which was always an article of clothing that was immediately tossed aside along with the wrapping paper, we'd hurry down to see what wonders Tommy and Irwin had amassed.

As soon as we walked in the door we were assaulted by a cacophony of mechanical and electronic sounds: motorized trucks whirring, machine guns blasting, robot voices screeching, trains chugging. Every toy would be operating at once, and Tommy and Irwin would be running around frantically trying to play with them all at the same time.

Why, I wondered, was life so unfair?

One Christmas Tommy got a pair of toy telephones that really worked! Tommy and Irwin lived in second-story apartments in adjacent buildings that were separated by an alley. So they got the inspired idea of stringing the phone wire across the alley so they could actually call each other between apartments. It worked perfectly, and my brother and I were so jealous of all the fun they were having that Christmas day that we almost stopped breathing.

The only drawback in the whole arrangement was that, because of the way the apartment windows faced each other, Tommy's phone was in his bedroom but Irwin's was in his parents'. And that very night Tommy called Irwin at 3:30 in the morning.

Irwin's father, more asleep than awake, picked up the phone. "Who is it?"

"Tommy. Is Irwin there?"

At which point Irwin's father woke up enough to realize that he was standing there in the middle of the night talking to a child on a toy phone, and he opened up the bedroom window and threw the thing directly out.

And that was the end of the smallest telephone monopoly in history.

Tommy and Irwin were always getting into trouble, and I was often along for the ride. But I never shared any of the blame because I was just a little kid—one of the few advantages inherent in that position.

In the back of Tommy's yard, at the fringe of a patch of woods, sat a wooden shack that had once been a large chicken coop. Tommy and Irwin cleaned the whole thing out, found an old rug to put on the floor, painted the walls, and created for themselves the neatest clubhouse the neighborhood had ever seen.

Everyone wanted to have access to it, but few did because Tommy and Irwin had adopted very high standards for membership. They wanted no dorkos around, so they wrote out membership cards for the privileged few. When they caught anyone in the clubhouse who didn't have a card, they beat the crap out of him.

Neighborhood kids could petition for membership, and every few days Tommy and Irwin held a meeting in the clubhouse during which they discussed the merits of the latest applicants. Their criteria were scientifically designed to screen out hidden bias, utilizing a list of dork factors that carried with them varying numbers of dork points. Tommy and Irwin evaluated an applicant by going through the list and then adding up the total number of points. If it exceeded the dork limit, which it did in almost every case, the applicant was rejected.

The three characteristics that carried the highest number of dork points were as follows:

(1) Is ugly
(2) Can't play sports
(3) Does good in school

Luckily, I never had to go through the review process myself because I was grandfathered in. But I did get my membership suspended a number of times when I was punished for various transgressions, such as not going on an errand when ordered.

Eventually they furnished the place with junk furniture they had scavenged, along with several Playboy magazines ferreted from garbage cans. And then one day they managed to steal a pack of cigarettes and brought it back to the clubhouse for a "smoking party."

I tried one and it was the most revolting thing I'd ever experienced: my throat burned, my eyes watered, I wanted to cough and throw up at the same time. Of course, I told Tommy and Irwin that it was great, and I copied them by smoking the thing right down to the filter. Then I went home to die.

Thirty minutes later the fire alarm went off, and soon I heard the fire trucks stopping somewhere very close. The air was sharp with the odor of something burning that shouldn't have been.

I ran outside and up the hill and, sure enough, the area behind Tommy's house was belching a plume of very black smoke. Tommy and Irwin had managed to burn down the clubhouse and the woods along with it. They escaped injury but not punishment: except for school, they were not allowed out of the house for a month.

Tommy and Irwin just had the extreme misfortune of being both mischievous and incapable of getting away with anything. There was that July day when Catskill was hosting a gigantic parade, held to celebrate a regional firemen's convention. Every non-Communist organization in the region marched in that parade: firemen, bands, women's auxiliaries, the National Guard, the VFW, Boy Scouts and Girl Scouts, Cub Scouts and Brownies, even local politicians (the most boring part of the whole parade). It was a wonder there was anyone left over to watch.

Irwin's apartment overlooked Main Street, and from the open windows we had a great view of the parade. As luck would have it, a vendor of helium balloons set up shop just below us. This was too much for Tommy and Irwin.

They armed themselves with rubber bands and paper clips and started picking off the guy's merchandise.

Pop! Duck down behind the window.

Pow! Duck down again.

The poor guy was bewildered. Surely his entire inventory of balloons couldn't be going bad all at once!

I felt privileged to witness this awesome display of power on the part of my two friends.

Then there was a loud knock at the door, and a few seconds later Irwin's mother came into the room with a policeman. He was carrying several spent paper clips in his hand, and they exactly matched the ones he found when he made Tommy and Irwin empty their pockets.

The policeman sent me home with a lecture about something he called "guilt by sociation." I didn't understand it. I just knew that it meant I wasn't going to jail.

Tommy and Irwin disappeared for another month.

With Big Kid friends like Tommy and Irwin, I was at their mercy at all times. On one occasion that proved to be a big advantage.

Catskill had its own daily newspaper, the *Daily Mail*. It was the quintessential small-town rag. The headline story was always something like "Firemen to Get New Pumper." The latest on the Cuban Missile Crisis would be found on page three under "Other News." (This sort of nearsighted provincialism is hardly limited to the minor media. We're all quite accustomed to nightly news lead-ins such as "One American was killed today in a massive earthquake in Ecuador. Three thousand others also perished.")

The most popular section of the paper was the "Chit Chat" column. This was written by a little old lady who gathered important social news from the area. A typical entry:

> Mrs. Clive Williams, the former Betty Schermann
> and wife of the late Clive Williams, former pro-
> prietor of the Nuts and Bolts hardware store on
> Main Street, motored to Leeds this Saturday af-

ternoon to have lunch with her sister-in-law, Mrs. Ray Williams, the former Ann Mulcahey and wife of Ray Williams, the former pastor of The Blessed Flock church and currently serving time in the Lewisberg Federal Penitentiary for a crime he did not commit.

They dined at the Rip Van Winkle Lodge and had a splendid view of the fall colors which so bless our area this time of year. Both ladies selected for their entree the hot roast beef sandwich on enriched white bread, accompanied by mashed potatoes and cole slaw. For dessert, Mrs. Clive Williams opted for the chocolate-pudding brownie, while Mrs. Ray Williams selected the homemade Cherry Pie Surprise.

Unfortunately, the Cherry Pie Surprise contained a pit, which broke Mrs. Williams's dentures. She managed to maintain her eternal good humor, however, and as she explained it to me, "At least it happened at the end of the meal."

One year the *Daily Mail*, in an effort to increase circulation, sponsored a subscription-selling contest. To enter you just had to pick up a sales kit, which contained order forms for subscriptions of one, two, and three years. Then you went out and tried to sell them. In addition to the grand prizes, every time you sold a subscription you earned a commission based on the total value of the sale.

The grand prize for the kid who sold the most subscriptions was a Huffy radio-bike. It was red and white, sporty as could be, with a radio actually built into the crossbar. For the duration of the contest the bike remained in a storefront window on Main Street, usually surrounded by a crowd of kids with faces pressed against the glass, each one boasting about how he was going to be the one to win it.

The grand prize for the adults was a car. We didn't much care about that. But the fact was that every single person in Greene County from the age of eight and up was trying to sell subscriptions to every other person in Greene County from the age of eight and up.

In a word, hopeless.

But Tommy, Irwin, and I didn't know this. So late one afternoon, all charged up with youthful optimism, we set out for a distant neighborhood to try our luck. (Our own neighborhood had already been sold dry, each kid having managed to sell a subscription to his own parents.)

We spread out and started knocking on doors, lots of doors. No luck. Everyone had already bought a subscription from a relative. Now we were discouraged. It was getting dark, and we had come to a cul-de-sac at the end of the street. Only three houses were left—two modern ranch-style homes and an old, haunted-looking Victorian mansion where Vincent Price probably lived.

Tommy and Irwin pulled rank on me. "We'll take those two houses here, and you have that one." They were laughing at me as they started off.

I was very scared as I walked onto the dark porch and rang the bell. A light came on in the hall, and someone called through the door: "Who is it?"

"W-would you like t-t-to buy a subscription to the *Daily Mail*?" I squeaked in a very weak voice.

The door opened and a beautiful young woman was standing there, smiling and saying, "Sure, come on in."

She led me to the kitchen, and I showed her the order form. My heart was thumping wildly from nervousness, excitement, and fear that I would say the wrong thing and blow the sale. I told her how much a one-year subscription cost and then, almost apologetically, showed her the prices for the two- and three-year deals.

"I'll take it for three years," she said.

I couldn't believe this was happening to me. We completed the forms and she gave me a check. I thanked her and just about ran out of the place before she could change her mind.

I bounded off the porch and started running to find Tommy and Irwin. I didn't have far to look because they were standing on the sidewalk in front of the house—where they'd been agonizing ever since they'd been immediately turned away at their modern ranch houses.

They knew that I was in that house, and they knew that it meant that I was either being murdered or making a sale. They were praying I wasn't making a sale.

"I sold a three-year one! I sold a three-year one!" I kept screaming. Seven dollars in commission (equal to about six months' allowance) and a leg up on that Huffy radio-bike!

We walked home, I chattering breathlessly about how smooth I'd been, and Tommy and Irwin looking like they were about to puke.

None of us sold another subscription after that. When the contest was over, I went down and proudly collected my commission. I pointedly asked Tommy and Irwin to come with me, but they had better things to do than to relive the worst mistake they'd ever made in their lives.

The meek may not inherit the earth, but they do sometimes make a sale.

5

Fun and Games

As a child, my time was devoted to two diametrically opposed types of activities: doing what my parents made me do, and having fun.

Among the former were going to school, doing homework, taking a bath, cleaning my room, eating beef tongue, and putting up with Randy. I longed for the day when I'd no longer have to do any of those things.

Having fun is the big payoff in being a kid; unlike adults, kids are good at it. At what point in our lives do most of us lose the ability to experience fun as a physical thrill in the gut? I think the effort to get it back is what pushes many adults into adventure sports and various Saturday night lunacies.

The kind of fun we had depended on the season, and we recognized only two: winter and summer.

Winter meant snow. Snow was exciting stuff, especially if it started to fall hard in the evening, holding out the promise of school cancellation the next day. Like Dust Bowl farmers praying for rain, every kid in town was constantly checking the skies and listening to the weather report. Hard-driving, small flakes were good, an indication that the storm was far from over. Larger, lazy-floating flakes were universally hated because they meant that the end was near.

Randy and I would get up anxiously several times during the night to peek outside. On rare occasions there'd be so much snow that we just knew there'd be no school, and we'd return to bed and sleep the sleep of the just.

More often we'd have to get up early to listen to the radio for school closings. It was total elation to hear "All Catskill schools are closed today," and total despair not to. But the worst was hearing that every school in the whole county was closed except for ours. Gut-wrenching misery was knowing that while we were trying to conjugate verbs in a musty, overheated classroom every other kid in the whole meaningful world was out playing in the snow.

Snow was the ultimate toy and it was free. We made snowballs out of it, wrestled in it, and sledded on it. We jumped into it, peed our names across it, and made forts out of it.

And we froze our asses off in it.

No matter how cold we got while playing outside, the idea of going inside never seemed to occur to us. But eventually darkness would begin to fall, or mothers would call, and then we had no choice but to go in. And that's when we paid the price for all the fun we'd had.

Once we entered the house, it quickly became apparent that we'd lost all feeling in our hands and feet. In order to remove a mitten we had to stick the hand under the opposite arm and pull the mitten off.

Then we had to attack those medieval, metal clasps on our galoshes, which were packed solid with ice and snow. Using our frozen hands like claws, we tried to pry them open. This was normally futile, so the next maneuver was to take one foot and step on the heel of the opposite boot and forcibly step out of it. We weren't supposed to do this because mothers claimed that it stretched the boots. This was obviously false because we did it every time, and they were still just as hard to get off the next time.

The next step was to remove our snow-crusted socks and jeans, stiff as lumber. Then it was time to sit next to the radiator and wait for the pain to begin.

Thawing out is like suffering a paper cut: you know you've been hurt and all you can do is wait for the pain to catch up to you. It always did. It started with a faint tingling in our otherwise leaden fingers and toes. The sensation grew more insistent and evolved into a dull ache. Then the ache moved into our very bones and ran right up into our temples and made our heads throb. By this time we were writhing on the floor with teeth clenched and eyes screwed shut, all linear thought obliterated.

Then slowly the aching in the bones began to subside and was replaced by liquid warmth. Our heads stopped throbbing, our muscles began to relax, and once again we could move our fingers and toes. We'd made it!

And we knew damned well that we were going to go out the next day and do it all over again.

Snowball fights, a popular winter pastime, are actually an early form of military training. The tactics we employed depended on whether the opponent was a friend or an enemy. If he was a friend, we made nice, light snowballs, the kind that would explode into a harmless spray if we got lucky enough to hit him. And we aimed for the body. If he was an enemy, we packed the snow hard and went for the head.

We'd usually end up injuring our friend in some freak fashion—snow would get in his eye or his ear, or he'd run into a telephone pole while trying to avoid one of our puffballs. On the other hand, our whistling iceballs never came close to the jerks we were really trying to clobber.

On one particular day of infamy, Randy and I were having a "friendly" snowball fight. He was in the lower yard, hiding behind a wall, and I held the high ground. He'd poke his head out to see where I was, jump out and heave a snowball, then duck back behind the wall. He kept repeating this maneuver: poke, jump, heave, duck. Poke, jump, heave, duck. It didn't take me long to get his rhythm. So I made two snowballs and when he jumped and heaved, I threw one at him. He ducked. And while he was still behind the wall, I tossed the second in a high, lazy arc, designed to intersect the coordinates of his face when he poked it out.

You need to believe me on this. I did not really want to hit him in the face with that snowball. If I could have guided it with remote control I would have made it miss (by a hair). Nor did I for a moment believe that I had a snowball's chance in hell of actually hitting him using that complicated strategy. If it had been an enemy, I wouldn't have wasted my time on such a hopeless scheme. I would have waited until I actually saw his ugly face, then thrown the iceball high and hard and hoped he hesitated with indecision just long enough for the missile to get in there and do some real damage.

This episode nicely illustrates one of the basic principles of life:

If you earnestly try to do something difficult in circumstances where some good would come of it, you won't get close. If you try that same thing in jest where it would cause great harm to succeed, it'll be a dead-on bull's-eye.

For reasons of both convenience and ego, I call this phenomenon "Denny's Law."

If it had been a mechanical target moving back and forth behind that wall and there was a million-dollar prize for hitting it, I could have thrown a ton of snowballs and still be trying.

As Randy poked his angelic little face out from behind the wall, the snowball's rainbow trajectory terminated abruptly between his eyes. He ran inside crying, and I got my backside heated up for hitting my little brother in the kisser with a snowball. And, believe it, an ass-whipping and a million dollars do not compare well.

You want another example? My friend Wayne and I were tossing a football around on the playground. We were about twenty yards apart and having trouble reaching each other at that. Meanwhile, a little neighbor girl was riding her bicycle around at the other end of the playground. She was calling Wayne names.

Wayne yelled, "You keep that up and I'm going to knock you right off that bike with this football." Wayne had to yell this because the little girl was about 100 yards away.

"Nah, nah, Wayne's a stupid head."

Wayne got a running start, reared back, and heaved the football high in the air in the general direction of the girl and the bike. The ball went sailing an amazing distance, but his aim was clearly off—as he knew full well it would be. He, of course, had no real intention of hitting the little girl and knocking her off the bike.

The little girl saw the brown projectile, panicked, and began pedalling furiously—toward the exact spot where it seemed the errant missile would eventually land. I watched as if in slow motion the awesome inevitability of it all got played out.

The football scored a direct hit and knocked her clean off the bike.

The little girl walked back home crying, her knees and her bike skinned. She told her parents how Wayne had threatened to throw the ball and knock her off her bike, and then had done exactly that. Her parents went to the police, the police went to Wayne's house, and Wayne failed to reappear until long after the little girl's wounds were healed.

Denny's Law had claimed another victim—Wayne. (The little girl deserved it.)

***

Some winter days were too miserable even for us to be outside. We then resorted to a healthy and educational alternative, which was to gather inside and play cards for money.

It all started innocently enough, playing marbles for "keepsies." When we outgrew that and had some money of our own, we graduated to poker, blackjack, and acey-deucy. We played for pennies and nickels, but that's all we had, so it was a big deal as far as we were concerned.

No matter what game we played, I lost money. I was the little scientist in the group, the crack mathematician. I always tried to play the odds, while my friends didn't know what odds were. They cleaned me out every time.

Then I saw an advertisement in a magic catalogue for a marked deck of cards; I immediately ordered it. When it arrived it was everything I had hoped for. The backs had an intricate design that looked the same on every card, but there was a slight variation which, when you learned what to look for, indicated what the card was.

I called my friend Keith to come down and play some blackjack. Keith always won money from me at cards, so he hurried right over. My plan was to astonish Keith by my extraordinary run of good fortune, win a tremendous amount of money from him, and then when he was totally dejected and broke, show him what was up, give him back his money, and have a good laugh about it. (This is the truth.)

Our normal stakes were five cents a hand. Rarely would anyone win more than forty or fifty cents in a session.

Keith and I played for a couple of hours, at the end of which I owed him three dollars.

When the deck is stacked against you there's nothing you can do, even when the deck is crooked. The only good that marked deck did me all afternoon was give me the privilege of knowing I was screwed a few seconds early.

Finally, my brilliant plan in ashes, I told Keith about the marked deck. He didn't believe me. (He obviously hadn't been given any reason to over the previous two hours.) So I showed him how I could read the cards from the back.

He got very mad and demanded his money. I tried to reason with him.

"Keith, this was just a joke. I wasn't going to take your money, so it's not fair to take mine."

He was unimpressed by my argument and demanded his money again. I didn't have the three dollars to give him. If it had been a real game I would have quit at the fifty-cent mark, which was about what I had to my name.

Keith was three years older than I was and six years bigger, and he wanted his money. So I pled bankruptcy and worked out a payment plan whereby over time I slowly paid him the money I had cheated myself out of.

There are a couple of traditional insults used to describe a luckless soul: "He couldn't get laid in a whorehouse with a pocketful of hundred-dollar bills," and "He couldn't win at cards with a marked deck."

At least the whorehouse is still an open question.

***

Nowadays, educational experts in this country are hot on the topic of self-esteem. Having pretty much failed to teach most of our young students to read and write, they have decided that the most important thing is to have our kids think the world of themselves. The schools seem to have done an admirable job at this, because several times a week the TV news will show some illiterate juvenile who has committed multiple homicide, and the kid always seems to be quite proud of himself.

I didn't need any lessons in self-respect, because the only problem I had with my ego was trying to keep it contained. No matter what activity I engaged in, even if I was trying it for the first time, I assumed that I was the best in the world at it until proven otherwise. Most of the time it was proven otherwise rapidly and convincingly, but chess was a different story.

We played a lot of chess during the winter; my friends and I had played for years and I remained unbeaten. I read chess books, memorized openings, and studied the games of old masters. I was even beating my dad, who had taught me the game years earlier. I began to imagine myself on the cover of *Life* magazine, confidently pondering a position on the chessboard.

On October 4, 1957, the Soviet Union successfully placed the first satellite in orbit, Sputnik I. This scared the hell out of the United States, because it threatened our technological superiority. And who knew what those Reds could do once they got up there? Maybe they could block the sun from shining on us and we'd have to pay by the minute for sunshine, like a big, solar peep show.

This marked the beginning of the space race, and our government started pouring money into scientific facilities and research. Initiatives were launched to push bright youngsters into the study of science and mathematics. I happened to be good at these things, and in the summer of 1963, between my junior and senior years of high school, I was selected to attend a seven-week science program sponsored by the National Science Foundation.

The program was held at Clarkson College, in northern New York, and fifty kids from around the country assembled there. Fifty boys. In fact, being male was a requirement. Perhaps it was felt that the presence of girls would distract us from our studies. This was undoubtedly correct.

The very first night, I was lying on my bed while replaying a game on the chessboard. My roommate, David, asked if I wanted to play a game. Of course I did.

He asked if I wanted to play for money. This was getting better by the moment. Of course I did.

We settled on a wager of a quarter and sat down to play. He seemed a bit better than my neighborhood friends, but I had no doubt about the outcome until I made a careless mistake and lost my queen. I hadn't played in a while and it had cost me. A quarter.

But now I was back in the groove and I was eager to win my quarter back. I was battling impressively in the next game when I made another careless mistake. Another quarter. I was humiliated and I was mad. I insisted on playing again. This time I didn't make any careless moves, but slowly he wore my position down until it was hopeless. I had now lost seventy-five cents at chess and absolutely couldn't believe it.

"Listen," David said, "I should tell you something. I came in second in the New York City Junior Chess Championship last year."

A thought immediately came to mind: if he thought that fact was relevant, why hadn't he mentioned it *before* he took my seventy-five cents?

Over the next few weeks we continued to play, though not for money. I didn't win a single game, no matter how well I thought I played. For competitive individuals, losing at chess is ego-crushing. Both players start with absolutely identical assets, and it is mind against mind. You cannot claim that your teammates let you down, or that your side of the board was muddy. You can't blame your loss on bad calls by the referee, or on fouls that went unseen. With all the usual excuses inoperative, you are put in the very painful position of having nobody to blame but yourself. For most people, these are uncharted waters.

Yet the loser at chess still has a last refuge. Since the defeat can't be blamed on anything external, the answer must be sought inside. And, yes, there we have it: *the loser didn't feel well.* In fact, one famous chess master complained that in his entire career he had never had the pleasure of beating a perfectly healthy opponent.

The trouble for me was that I was feeling fine. So I was forced to conclude that I was not the best chess player in the world: since David had come in second in his championship, and he was beating me, I was probably about third.

As I lay on my bed one evening with the chessboard, trying to come up with a new opening that would befuddle David, he asked if I wanted to play. His invitation made me happy because he hadn't seemed anxious to play in a while, and I was starting to suspect that he no longer considered me a worthy opponent. But it was now apparent that I was being paranoid.

I told him yes and asked if he wanted to play on his side of the room or mine.

"That's okay, you stay over there and I'll stay here," he said, as he perused a magazine.

"But you can't see the board from there," I pointed out helpfully.

"Right."

Now I understood. I had read about chess masters who could play "blindfold" chess. Out of sight of the board, they call out their moves using a common chess notation, and their opponents make that move for them on the board. When the "sighted" opponent makes his own move on the board, he calls it out using the notation and the blindfolded player makes that move on his mental chessboard.

I knew, intellectually, that some people could do this—but I couldn't actually *believe* it until I saw it.

David told me to take white and move first.

"Pawn to king-4," I said, as I moved my pawn to the corresponding square.

"Pawn to king-4," he said, and I moved his pawn accordingly.

We each made a few more moves, at which point I was completely certain that he could no longer accurately visualize the position on the board.

"Queen to rook-5," I said. This put my queen in a very strong position, with the minor drawback that he could immediately capture it with his knight. He could, that is, if he could only see what was going on.

"You idiot," David said charitably, "Knight takes queen."
I now believed.

"All right," I said, "That was just a test. Now let's play for real."

We did and I lost, and I kept on losing over the next several weeks. I found that his game wasn't quite as strong blindfolded, but plenty strong enough to beat me every single time. We were in the middle of one such game, he watching TV with his back to me, and I staring at a complex position on the board, trying to calculate the lines of play that would follow each of my possible moves. David got impatient with the amount of time I was taking; he told me he was going downstairs for a milkshake.

I liked that idea because I was confident that the break in concentration would cost him the game. I had the advantage of staring at real pieces on a real board, but if I looked away for even a few seconds and then looked back, it took me some time to reset it all. He didn't have a real board to begin with, and now he was going to take a ten-minute break. I was looking forward to my first win, and by that point I didn't care how I got it.

I made my move and saw that it was good.

David returned and sat back down in front of the TV, slurping his milkshake.

"Did you move yet, I hope?" he asked.

"Yep. Bishop to knight-5." I tried to keep a flat tone, to hide my excitement.

"You mean you took all that time to make that crap move? Now you're dead meat."

"What the hell are you talking about?" I honestly wanted to know.

With his back still to the board, he proceeded to go through the next several moves, the outcome of which was dead meat rotting on my bed. I could only follow his analysis, of course, by moving the pieces around on the board, but I saw that he was right.

I didn't play chess again for years—it took that long for the wounds to heal.

David told me that in the city he had plenty of friends his age who were just as good as he was. (Was that supposed to make me feel better?) Sometimes, when a board was not available or practical, such as when riding the bus or while at work, he and a friend would play a game with no board at all. That is, they both played blindfolded. (This is not recommended for sore losers who resort to "accidentally" knocking over the board to escape a losing game.)

I thought a lot about David and blindfold chess after that, and I came to realize that I, dependent upon the physical pieces and board, was really the one playing at a disadvantage, not David. For me, the chess set was a physical crutch that I needed to keep my inferior chess intellect limping along. David didn't need the mediation of physical tokens.

Over the years I've been confronted with the same phenomenon in science, mathematics, music, and other games such as bridge. And I was forced to conclude that I wasn't the best in the world at these, either.

But, just between you and me, I really wasn't feeling that well.

***

Winter was fun, but summer was better. Absence may make the heart grow fonder, but not when it comes to school. (Proverbs still confuse me. Which is it: "Absence makes the heart grow fonder," or "Out of sight, out of mind"? "A penny saved is a penny earned," or "You can't take it with you"? "Patience is a virtue," or "He who hesitates is lost"? Let's just make life simpler and replace all the proverbs with "If you want to do it, that's terrific.")

Just as water in the form of snow played such an important role in our winter activities, water was central to much of our summer fun: we swam in it almost every afternoon.

Most of us learned to swim in a country creek called Slippery Rock, located in Leeds. One side of the creek was private farmland, but the other was owned by an old Dutch family, the Van Vechtens, and they welcomed the public. They had a little snack bar on the grounds and did very well selling soda, candy, hot dogs, and hamburgers.

The snack bar was run by Mrs. Van Vechten, a kindly, white-haired old lady who made the best hot dog relish I've ever had, even to this day. We'd load our hot dogs as high as possible with that delicious relish and then leave a trail behind us as we tried to walk and eat at the same time. Dessert was a frozen Milky Way on a stick, washed down with a Yoo-Hoo. That was living.

The name Slippery Rock was no joke. To get into the creek, it was necessary to negotiate a steeply inclined, moss-covered, rocky bank, just below the waterline. It extended for about ten feet until the bottom leveled out, and it was as slippery as ice.

There were three ways to manage it. The macho way was to get into a crouch and water-ski down. That's how we did it, of course.

The chicken's way (adults, babies, and sissies) was to slide down while sitting.

The third way was employed only by city tourists who were visiting Slippery Rock for the first time. This was to walk into the water in a normal fashion and come crashing down on their butts in a shower of water.

To us, this ranked as the funniest thing in the world. It was a great pastime to watch as the unsuspecting boarder families came down the hill toward the creek, spread their blankets, and enthused about the beauty of the place. What a tremendous feeling of power to see a disaster in the making, knowing that we could prevent it, but doing absolutely nothing. Instead, we made bets about who was going to venture into the water first. It was usually the father, who would amble down to the water's edge, belly sagging over a knee-length, baggy, plaid swimsuit. In he would go, and then down he would go, as we rolled around on the grass, choking on our Yoo-Hoos.

The great thing about Slippery Rock for kids was that it was extremely shallow at the lower end of the creek and gradually got deeper upstream. So we learned to swim at the shallow end, and as we got older and became better swimmers we gradually moved farther upstream. Conspicuously spreading your towel along the part of the creek that everyone knew was over your head was a powerful statement. It was rather like a country boy's bar mitzvah.

Kids seem to be genetically programmed to think that the deeper the water, the harder it is to swim in it. Conversations about it went like this:

"Last week I swam in Lake Taconic and the water was eight feet deep."

"So what? I swam in Green Lake and it's fifteen feet deep there."

"Big deal. I swam in the ocean and my father says the ocean doesn't even have a bottom."

"You did not!"

Numerous times I tried to convince my friends that once you were swimming, it felt the same no matter how deep the water was. This was so obviously false to them that they concluded I was totally stupid.

Our other swimming hangout was the Catskill public swimming pool. This was a huge concrete pool, with three sections of different depths: three, five, and eight feet. The deep end had two diving boards—a low board and a high board. A multi-tiered fountain that looked like a giant wedding cake was the centerpiece of the pool. The snack bar served great hot dogs and hamburgers (although the relish fell short of Mrs. Van Vechten's). For thirty-five cents admission we could spend the whole day in that kid's paradise.

Our favorite game there was "submarine." In order to play, a target was required. The most attractive target was a boarder asleep on a rubber air-mattress in the five-foot-deep area.

The object was to swim underwater from the deep end, which was our base of operations, get under the target, unscrew the air valve, and return underwater to base. A successful mission ended with us watching the mattress and its still-sleeping occupant suddenly fold up like a jackknife and sink. We'd quickly duck underwater ourselves so we could laugh and scream without giving ourselves away. The surface of the water above us would look like a scuba tank had just exploded.

For the rest of the afternoon we innocently went about our business, as the irate boarder tried to learn the identity of the saboteur. We always seemed to end up as the prime suspects, but nobody could ever prove anything.

***

Another popular summer activity was building and racing "hot rods." These were soapboxes built from scrap lumber, orange crates, and wagon wheels. We'd pair off and race them down the hilly, back streets in our neighborhood.

Our earliest versions had no steering wheels; instead, we used our feet to push the front axle left or right. This worked well, but it lacked realism. Eventually we progressed to steering wheels, which were attached to the front axle with ropes and pulleys. But no matter how we designed the steering mechanism, it always had the same flaw: we had to turn the wheel in the opposite direction from the one in which we wanted to steer. Eventually we just got used to dyslexic driving.

But when an unexpected situation arose which required reflex action we'd steer the "wrong" way every time. Split-second instinct will not permit you to turn the steering wheel *toward* something that's about to kill you.

Once I was barreling down the hill when a huge German shepherd bolted out from between two parked cars to my left and gave chase, its snarling face inches from my own. I instinctively jerked the wheel to the right and swerved left directly into him, knocking him head over paws. He kept right on running into the woods, no doubt convinced that he had picked on an animal crazier than he was. With a steering wheel that operated correctly I would have swerved to the right, as was my intention, and he'd have caught me and used my head as a chew toy.

One day a kid from another neighborhood showed up with a sleek, black hot rod. It had a steering wheel that miraculously worked the way it should. But since the steering mechanism was hidden underneath an aerodynamically shaped hood (no orange crate for this kid), we couldn't see how it was done. And he was not about to tell us.

He boasted that he had built the racer himself, but we couldn't accept this. We just knew we were as mechanically advanced as kids could be (the steering problem notwithstanding), so how could this twerp come up with a racer that made ours look like trash heaps on wheels? We concluded that his father must have built it. That's why it looked so good, was so much faster, and steered correctly. That was the only explanation. And here he was, trying to pass it off as his own creation and showing us up.

We held a conference to discuss how we were going to handle this assault on our self-esteem. We decided that we had no choice—there was only one rational course of action.

We marched en masse up to this intruder and explained to him that he had two minutes to disappear, and that if he ever brought his "sissy wagon" to our neighborhood again we'd bust it up, with him in it.

He was gone in one minute, and with our egos restored, we resumed racing our wrong-steering, nonaerodynamic contraptions. But the truth was that that day marked the beginning of the end of our hot rod phase. We could never feel entirely good about our little vehicles again.

We all knew full well that adults could build fantastic things like cars and skyscrapers and jet planes. But those were part of the grown-up world.

Hot rods were part of our world. We took scraps that the adults didn't want and with our own creativity built the ultimate toys. It made us feel independent, capable. But now the adults had intruded on our world and built something that, by comparison, showed us that we were nothing but little kids after all.

A few years later the first annual Soap Box Derby was held in Catskill. All the kids that I knew who entered had handy fathers with workshops. I went to watch it. The race cars all looked sleek and beautiful; they all steered the right way. At the age of ten I can remember feeling that the times were leaving me behind.

Indulge me here for a moment—I want to whine about something: Adults have no business meddling in children's play. Whenever they do, they ruin it. We were lucky in that, once we went out to play, we were completely autonomous of adults. We organized our own games on our own schedule, picked our own teams, made our own rules, and settled disagreements ourselves. We walked or biked wherever we went, and no kid ever wanted to be seen being dropped off by his mom or dad, for fear of being (justifiably) labeled a pansy-ass.

Our only recreational activity in which adults held sway was Little League baseball, and Little League baseball was (and is) a tragic mutation of childhood play. Children of that age should not be pressured to win, yelled at for missing a play, or segregated by talent. Our own coach checked our eyes before each game. If they were bloodshot, he concluded that we had been swimming that day, wasting valuable energy that should have been saved to help make him a winner, and he benched us for the game.

Then, too, we have the spectacle of the game being held up while the coaches and parents berate, or assault, the umpires, as the players stand by and observe what will be expected of them when they become role models themselves.

Kids are sent out to knock on doors to sell their mandatory allotment of raffle tickets, in order to bring in enough revenue to support the sagging weight of the bureaucracy the adults have created for "the benefit of the kids."

And, of course, some adults, for the benefit of the kids, bring cheating into the mix, using players who are overage or otherwise ineligible because of residency requirements and the like.

Adults can serve a useful role by helping with the instructional aspects of sports, but they should leave the organization of the games to the kids. Let the kids pick their own teams for each game, and let them be their own umpires and referees, just like kids used to do before computers were necessary to keep track of their scheduled activities. They'll have more fun and they'll learn a lot more, not just about sports.

So here's my proposal. Do away with all these leagues run by adults and let the kids regain dominion over their own play. Failing that, then let's be fair about it: Put the kids in charge of all the amateur, adult sports leagues. And bench any player with beer on his breath.

***

Toy guns played an important role in our childhood play. As we got older, our weaponry became increasingly sophisticated.

Our first guns were little plastic toys that had no moving parts, so we'd have to run around making the shooting noises ourselves. Some kids were better at this than others. The best among us could even imitate the sound of a bullet ricochetting off rock. We got this from the cowboy movies, where every time someone fired a shot it ricochetted off a rock. It didn't seem to matter that this happened even in the desert, with nary a rock in sight.

As we got older we graduated to real weapons: cap guns. Now we felt more like our heroes in the movies. We didn't have to go around making silly noises with our mouths. The guns sounded real, they smoked, and they required loading.

We had great range wars in our neighborhood, with a dozen kids running through the streets and yards (especially the Rivers's yard), all with cowboy hats and holsters, screaming and firing our guns. The smell of gunpowder filled the air, and each one of us was the toughest sum-bitch in the valley.

Unfortunately, endless arguments ensued over who shot whom. The only time an argument didn't occur was when we were lucky enough to sneak up right behind someone and shoot him in the back. But this was rare.

Mostly, the arguments went like this:

"I got you. You're dead."

"You did not. I ducked behind the tree before you shot."

"You're full of it. You were right out in the open when I fired. I aimed right at your chest. Everyone saw it."

"You just grazed me. I can still fight."

Of course, nowadays kids use real guns, so there's no longer any need for such arguments.

In the mid-1950s Hollywood supplanted cowboy movies with war movies, and Audie Murphy became our new hero. Playing cowboy was baby stuff—we wanted to kill Germans and Japs.

So apparently did millions of other kids around the country, because the toy industry responded with a wide variety of battery-operated weapons of war. These guns moved us into the big leagues. They issued sparks and light flashes and endless barrages of terrifically loud reports.

We waged war in the schoolyard woods. We'd split up into two teams, and the first team was given a head start to go into the woods and hide. Then the second team would move in and the battle would begin. I had a machine gun with a tripod, and I'd set up a hidden nest and just mow 'em down. The noise emanating from those woods must have given flashbacks to every World War II veteran living in the area.

One of my friends had two genuine hand grenades, supposedly "duds," given to him by his veteran uncle. They were very heavy and reminded us of metal pineapples. He hooked them to his belt and when he got pinned down, he lobbed them at his attackers. If a grenade landed near one of us, we were "blown up"—unless we could grab it in a hurry and throw it back at him, like Audie did. (Now, whenever I read about World War II munitions still posing a danger in the European countryside, I think back to those "dud" grenades.)

Barely five years later some of my fellow soldiers who had fought it out in those woods were doing it again in Vietnam.

***

Though Catskill was a rural area with numerous farms in the vicinity, I only went horseback riding once in my life. This might be shocking to some, but what was really shocking was what happened to me on that one occasion.

My friend Wayne was an excellent rider, having spent many summers on his cousin Sammy's ranch in the mountains. Wayne and Sammy were at loose ends in Catskill one weekend and decided to go riding at a local dude ranch. The owner knew them well and always let them go out alone without the usual guide.

They invited me to go with them, and though I was not chomping at the bit to accept, I agreed. Riding certainly looked easy enough when the cowboys did it on TV and in the movies. I had good balance and was not a fearful person; I saw no reason why I wouldn't be world class by the end of the ride.

As we pedalled our bikes up to the ranch, Wayne and Sammy gave me my instructions. If the owner knew I'd never ridden before, he'd make a guide go with us. Wayne and Sammy did not want a guide. Therefore, it was up to me to make the owner think I knew what I was doing.

They explained to me that when I was assigned a horse, the first thing I should do was to check the cinch to make sure it was snug. That was a sure sign of someone who knew horses.

Then I was to grab the bridle and stare into the horse's eyes for a few seconds. This would establish my dominance over the critter and erase any remaining doubt in the owner about my credentials.

They explained how to mount up and hold the reins, and how to adjust to the rhythm of the horse so that my butt wasn't going down when the saddle was coming up.

And, finally, they admonished me never to hold on to the saddle horn, because that was the unmistakable sign of a beginner.

All of this sounded straightforward, and I envisioned myself galloping over the hills, with Wayne and Sammy choking on my dust.

When we arrived, Wayne and Sammy introduced me to the owner and explained that I was a riding instructor from Virginia. He greeted me warmly and then walked us to the barn. Because we were all skilled horsemen, he passed by the nags that were normally used for lugging around the dead weight of novices.

"Here, these three are good ones. Have fun out there."

Wayne and Sammy picked out their horses and pointed out mine. I strode over and made a big deal of checking the cinch, but by that time the owner had left so my performance went unappreciated.

My posse mounted up and I did the same. I couldn't believe how high I was off the ground, or how big that damned horse was. I could see right away that falling off might be a poor idea.

I didn't notice any obvious movement on the part of Wayne and Sammy, but for some reason their horses started walking out of the barn. Mine didn't. I patted him a few times on the side and shook the reins, but he just stood there.

"Kick him in the side with your heels," Wayne yelled.

I didn't at all like the idea of kicking an animal for no reason. I gave a few weak jabs with my heels and tried to make that weird clicking noise that Roy Rogers and the Lone Ranger always did. My horse continued to ignore me.

Wayne and Sammy rode back into the barn. They were nervous now that the owner might see what was happening and somehow conclude that I was a greenhorn.

"You've got to really kick him. You won't hurt him."

I really kicked him, but he still didn't budge.

"Wayne, I don't get it," I said in frustration. "I'm doing everything you're telling me to, but he just won't move."

"It's because he knows you're a beginner, so he's just going to fuck with you."

I was pretty insulted—how did the horse know I was just a beginner? I was sitting tall in the saddle, definitely not holding on to the horn, and kicking him for all I was worth. What was not to like?

Finally Wayne grabbed the reins and started to lead my horse out of the barn. My horse continued to follow and I took the reins before we exited the barn. If the owner was watching now, he'd have seen three hardened rancheros heading out to the range for a workout.

We went out to a large field that was ringed by a riding trail. We made several circuits, with me following behind, gradually increasing speed as I picked up the technique and grew more confident. Eventually Wayne and Sammy were going at a full gallop, and my horse followed suit, though we were losing ground. I hadn't yet grabbed onto the horn and I was extremely pleased with myself.

Wayne and Sammy continued to gain on me, but my horse was on his own—I was just along for the ride. Eventually Wayne and Sammy were no longer ahead of me—they were across from me, on the other side of the field. And my horse did a little geometry and realized that it was stupid for him to continue chasing his friends around the perimeter of the field when he could save a lot of time and energy by cutting directly across.

He veered sharply and lit off at a gallop across the field. The main problem with this was that the field was extremely rough, with ruts, rocks, bushes, and holes, and was marked with signs indicating OFF-LIMITS FOR RIDING. This didn't faze my horse, who was bounding around and over the obstacles with enthusiasm. It did faze me, however, because I was now hanging completely off the side of the horse, one foot totally free of the stirrup, both hands locked in a death grip on the forbidden horn. From that angle I had a great view of the ground whizzing by and the horse's flying front hoof, which was missing my nose by inches.

At that point I had completely stopped worrying about the owner looking out and realizing that I was a fraud, because if he had he could conclude nothing other than that I was a trick rider practicing my moves. I was now worried about something more elemental: my ass.

Wayne and Sammy had stopped their horses to enjoy the show. When my horse saw this, he relaxed a bit and slowed down, and I was able to pull myself back up and regain the saddle. When we got over to them, my friends were laughing so hard they had to dismount. This seems to be a peculiarity of males, both young and old: watching a friend come very close to violent death is nothing less than hysterically funny.

After that, I saw no point in ever going riding again. I figured that in thirty minutes I had done just about everything it's possible to do on a horse, and I had nothing left to prove. Wayne and Sammy agreed completely.

***

Another vivid memory from those childhood summers is Bill Straub's Day Camp. Bill Straub had been a promising minor-league baseball player, but a badly broken hand ended his career. So he started another, that of high school teacher and coach; and in the summers he and his wife ran a very popular day camp for boys, where all manner of sports and crafts were taught.

Coach Straub's idea of an affectionate gesture was to pick a camper up by the ear. If he was in an especially amiable mood, half the kids in camp would be walking around holding the sides of their heads, some in pain and others in self-defense.

He had a booming voice that grew louder the farther away from him you got. And he seemed to see everything, even if he wasn't in the vicinity. You could get away with nothing. Say you were at the archery range by yourself and you broke one of the ten million arrows that were there. Then let's say you threw the arrow into the woods, far into the woods, so you wouldn't have to explain to Coach how you had screwed up and broken one of his ten million arrows. (This is a purely hypothetical example, you understand.)

When the period was over you walked back to the main assembly area, affecting your most nonchalant air. You sat on the ground in the middle of sixty other kids, and you looked up to find Coach staring directly into your eyes with a diamond-cutting glare that left absolutely no room for doubt. He knew!

For the rest of the day you lived in fear. Maybe he would say something to you like "How'd it go at the archery range today?" and you knew he was testing your nerve. Maybe he would say nothing but continue to glare at you all afternoon until you had to summon every strand of your immoral fiber to keep from crying out, "I'm sorry, Coach! I didn't mean to do it."

Coach had little patience for whiners, crybabies, or people who lacked "hustle" (which, for Coach, was the absolute worst thing you could say about anyone). If Coach knew you didn't like a certain sport, he'd make you play it all day long. If you were afraid of the water, you can bet you'd be spending more time in the lake than a lily pad.

And I was afraid of the water. Or, more accurately, I was afraid of what was under the water. The lake at the camp had a sandy bottom and it was mined with sharp roots. We good swimmers got into the habit of diving in as soon as the water was deep enough, to avoid walking on that treacherous lake bottom any more than necessary.

Toward the end of one summer we were having our camp-wide competition and it was time for the "watermelon race." The rules were simple: Coach divided the camp into two teams, each one facing the other while standing waist-deep at opposite ends of the shallow-water area, which was bounded by rope. Then Coach would take a large greased watermelon and throw it in the water between the teams. The object was for a team to get the watermelon across the rope boundary that served as the goal line of the other team.

Any means of moving the watermelon was permitted: running with it, swimming with it, or throwing it. And any means of stopping the watermelon from being moved was permitted: tackling, wrestling, or dunking.

I wanted no part of this. I didn't care what anybody said—I wasn't going to play that stupid game. As the teams marched dutifully into the water, I went up to Coach to reason with him.

"Coach, I don't want to play this game. Please can I just sit and watch?"

He actually looked hurt. "What are you talking about? Why don't you want to play?"

"Well, there are a lot of sharp roots in there, and I'm afraid I'm going to cut my foot."

How could I know that trying to opt out of a manly sport for fear of injury was like trying to convince the Lord not to send you to hell because you're prone to heat rash?

He picked me up by the ear and carried me down to the water's edge.

"You get in there and play. Your team needs you."

Well, you can lead a camper to water but you can't make him chase the watermelon. I had another ace up my bathing trunks. I decided that I was just going to lie low in the water, splash around a lot, and get lost in all the commotion. I damned sure wasn't going to go running around in there and risk amputating my foot.

The contest was an evenly matched free-for-all with yelling, splashing, and choking. I spent my time out of harm's way, yet trying to blend in. After all, I had to come out of the water eventually, and Coach would be waiting for me if he noticed that I wasn't fighting for the win.

Suddenly the watermelon came shooting out of a pack of combatants and landed two feet in front of me. My team was screaming, "Get it, Denny! Get it!"

My competitive instincts took over and without thinking I took a lunging step toward the watermelon—and stepped on a root and cut my foot wide open.

I limped out of the water and sat down on the beach. Coach was coming straight for me, homing in on my ear, when he saw the bloody mess that only moments earlier had been my foot.

"I told you," I kept repeating to him like a mantra as he administered first aid.

Meanwhile, back in the water, sixty crazed adolescents continued to swarm over that lake bottom without a scratch, until finally the badly battered watermelon got pushed over the rope and my team was declared the winner.

My teammates gathered around as Coach put the finishing touches on my bandage.

"Man, you really went for that thing!"

"You would have scored if you didn't cut yourself!"

I was the war hero, injured in battle. I had given my all for a just cause.

But I came away from that day with two very troublesome suspicions. One was that adults in the position of authority could be very wrong. The other was that maybe fearing something makes it all the more probable that it will occur.

But not even that experience prepared me for the day I killed the chicken.

If the weather was nasty on a camp day, Coach bused us to Bigelow Hall, a huge wooden structure housing a basketball court and a second-floor hall that we used for crafts. Bigelow Hall days were fun. We played volleyball, basketball, and "steal the bacon." We shot air rifles at paper targets at the other end of the court, and we worked on craft projects like straw baskets, etched metal trays, and braided whistle-chains.

One rainy day a few of us were standing on the second floor, looking through an open window into the adjoining yard, where we spied some kind of a metal tank. And, for some fateful reason, several rocks lay on the floor near where we stood.

Throughout history, the combination of kids, rocks, and metal tanks has always meant big trouble. That day in Bigelow Hall was no different.

With Coach safely downstairs excoriating some innocent who had just double dribbled, we took turns chucking the stones out the window at the tank. We were almost out of stones when I finally hit the tank dead center and made it ring like a Chinese gong. We ducked back away from the window to avoid being seen. I was quite proud of myself.

Ten minutes later a shabbily dressed woman came barging through the front door of Bigelow Hall and made straight for the only adult there—Coach. We did not know this woman and we could not hear what she was saying. But we could very clearly see the look on Coach's face. It was a look that did not promise good things.

The woman huffed out. Coach blew his whistle—it was deafening in that building—and yelled for everyone to drop what he was doing that instant and assemble on the basketball floor. We quickly gathered around him and sat down cross-legged. For what seemed like hours he just kept scrutinizing us one by one, as if he were looking for something very specific.

Then he spoke very slowly.

"Who killed the chicken?"

What the hell was he talking about? We had all been inside all morning, and none of us had ever seen a barnyard animal in Bigelow Hall.

"Who threw the stone at that chicken?"

I suddenly had to go to the bathroom real bad.

"The woman who lives in back saw a kid in a red shirt throw a stone out the window. It bounced off a tank and into her chicken coop. It killed her chicken."

I tried to keep from glancing down at my fire-engine-red shirt. Instead, I looked around and counted seven other campers wearing shirts that could be fairly described as red. They were innocent, but they looked as scared as I felt. I knew without a doubt that before the day was out I was going to be as dead as that chicken. I imagined how the story would read the next day in the *Daily Mail*:

LOCAL YOUTH DIES IN FREAK MISHAP

Dennis Fried, age 10, lifelong resident of Catskill, lost his life yesterday when he fell out of a second-story window and landed on a chicken. Coach Bill Straub, proprietor of the day camp where the accident occurred, was quoted as saying he believed the boy fell from the window while throwing stones at the chicken. Investigators say that in addition to being crushed, the chicken did show signs of injury which could have been caused by a projectile.

There were no witnesses to the tragedy. At the time of the accident, all the other campers were downstairs, where Coach Straub had instructed them to lie face down with their arms over their heads for a short rest period. Coach went upstairs to check on Fried, who had been left there as a punishment for misbehavior, and that's when the tragedy was discovered.

In lieu of flowers, it is asked that donations be
made in Dennis's name to the local chapter of
the SPCA.

Coach spoke again. "Before you all leave today, I want to know
who threw that stone. Now go back to what you were doing."

I walked like a zombie back to the craft area and tried to
continue weaving my basket. Three hours remained before the
bus would take us home. If I could make it until then, I might
have a chance. I started counting the minutes like a prisoner
counts the days.

Every time I saw Coach talking to a kid, my blood froze.
Was the kid turning me in? Was this the end of the road? But the
afternoon crept along, and still I was alive.

Finally it came time to line up for the ride home. I kept watching Coach out of the corner of my eye to see if he was going to
make a last-second lunge for me.

Into the bus, door closing, bus lurching to a start, rolling
down the country road as Bigelow Hall disappeared in the distance.

I was still scared to death. Now I was watching through the
back window for Coach's car. If he found out the truth after I
left, he would chase the bus down and drag me off it.

It never happened. The bus arrived on my street and I jumped
out and ran into the house. I flopped on the couch and expelled
the breath I had been holding since that woman came bursting
through the front door of Bigelow Hall. I had defied the odds
and won; I had killed a chicken at Bill Straub's Day Camp and
lived to tell about it.

That chicken undoubtedly lacked hustle.

6

Sardo

As our friend Andy was preparing his bike for his daily paper route, he felt something tug at the back of his leg. He turned to see a very small puppy looking up at him. The dog was bright white except for a brown spot on his back and one ear that was brown at the tip. One ear stood up ramrod straight, while the brown-tipped one flopped over, as if the extra color added too much weight.

Andy bent over to pet him. The dog was wary at first, but his desire for friendship quickly overcame his fear. Andy searched for a collar under the fluffy fur but found none.

After a few minutes Andy reluctantly jumped on his bike and started off; his customers were used to getting their papers on time, and he didn't like to disappoint them. The little dog took off after him. He couldn't keep up with the bike, but he kept right on chasing anyway. Andy stopped occasionally to let him catch up, petting him for a few seconds and then resuming his ride, the dog in hot pursuit.

Ninety minutes and several miles later they arrived back at Andy's house. Andy went in and brought out a bowl of milk, which the dog lapped up without taking a breath. Then Andy went in for his own supper, and when he came back out the dog was waiting for him.

Andy couldn't sleep much that night, worrying about the dog that he didn't expect to see again. He got up extra early and rushed outside. His little friend was there to greet him. No question about it now: the dog was his responsibility. Andy tied a rope loosely around the dog's neck for a leash and led him down to introduce him to Randy and me. In a few minutes the dog had two more friends.

Our parents contacted the police and the pound, but neither had any reports of a lost dog. We were told that we could keep him, unless someone claimed him within seven days, or we could turn him in to the pound.

Andy pleaded with his parents to let him keep the dog, but to no avail. It was now up to Randy and me. We got the same answer. When my mother and father were newlyweds they had owned a dog which they loved dearly. One day it just disappeared from their backyard and they never found it. Heartbroken, they agreed never to own a pet again; they didn't want to revisit that sadness a second time. They also knew the amount of work involved in caring for a pet and were well aware that the bulk of it would fall to them, in spite of our assurances otherwise. So the answer was no.

They agreed, however, to let us keep him in our enclosed backyard for the week's waiting period, rather than send him to the pound right away. This, of course, was their big mistake.

Aside from some trees, there was no shelter in our yard, so we decided to build a doghouse. We gathered some scrap lumber and other building material, borrowed some tools from Andy's father, and spent an afternoon building the thing from scratch. We had tied the little dog to a tree, and it barked excitedly the whole time, like an anxious homeowner watching his dream house being constructed.

Kids like to call each other names, especially nonsense names they've made up themselves. For reasons lost to history, the three of us had recently been calling one another "dumb sardo" at every opportunity. As we built the doghouse, Andy would drop the hammer and be a "dumb sardo." I would break a nail and be nothing but a "dumb sardo." "Dumb sardo" Randy would bring us the wrong board.

The dog, of course, was now one of us, so when his barking became especially shrill it was natural enough to tell him to "Shut up, you dumb sardo." By the end of the afternoon he had a name: Sardo.

He also had himself a canine palace. The house was huge, with a shingle roof, overhanging eaves, tile interior, and wall-to-wall carpeting. It also weighed a ton and took the three of us all our might to move it.

We couldn't wait to see how Sardo looked in his new house, so we led him over and tried to coax him in. He wanted no part of it.

Finally we picked him up and put him in. He came running right out. We tried it again. He was out like a shot. All that work for nothing. We thought maybe he didn't like the carpet we'd picked out.

For the next two days we tried everything to get him to stay in his house. We threw dog biscuits in. He'd run in, grab the treat, and run right back out. We crawled into the house our-selves and called him. He'd just look at us like we were nothing but dumb sardos.

On the third night a hard rain began to fall. We ran to the window and looked out into the backyard. And there, barely vis-ible in the back of the doghouse, was a white ball of fur. The little hobo had come home!

The days ticked off and we grew more and more nervous because we knew that at the end of the week, if no one had claimed Sardo, a decision would have to be made. And the deci-sion was not going to be ours.

But we had noticed a hopeful sign. One day we looked out the window and saw our father playing with the dog. Sardo would jump onto his leg with all fours and then run around in a big circle as my father engaged in a mock chase. My father had no chance of catching him, so he'd give up and stop. Sardo would jump on him again, and away they went one more time.

Old-time salesmen often say that getting a prospect to touch the product is tantamount to making the sale. Sardo was doing one heck of a job selling himself. The next day my father and mother took Sardo for a walk. This was getting better all the time!

Then the week was up. We were afraid to ask the crucial question, so we didn't. A few more days went by. My father was now playing with Sardo on his lunch hour, and my mother was joining them for an early evening walk.

So it was that at the dinner table a few days later, my father, as he was buttering a slice of bread, casually remarked, "You can keep the dog." We jumped up screaming and ran out to tell Sardo, but he acted as if he already knew. A few weeks later we asked my father if he would sell Sardo for a million dollars and he said no. If that wasn't completely true, I don't think it missed by more than a few hundred thousand.

Sardo ("Sard" for short) quickly became a member of the family, although he wasn't allowed inside our house for many months. All he knew was that we disappeared through that back door at night and reappeared from it in the morning, and he couldn't stand to think that something was going on in there that he wasn't party to. He'd stand by the back door and bark and whine as only a puppy can, and when he got no response he'd slink off under a tree and look highly insulted.

One day my mother announced that we could let him in for a few minutes to see how he would act. After all, we had no way of knowing if he had ever been inside a human house before. We opened the back door and called him. He came running and stopped abruptly at the threshold, even though we had the door wide open for him. Old habits die hard.

114

"Come on, Sard," we urged. He looked at us as if to say, "Are you quite sure about this?"

"Sard, come on!"

Now he knew we were serious and he bolted in like a flash. He ran right through the den, through the living room, and came to a dead end in the kitchen. He made a skidding 180 on the linoleum floor and ran back through the living room and into the den. Turned on a dime and did the whole tour again at warp speed, ears pinned back flat on his head and barking like a machine gun. And again. All we could see was a white streak every thirty seconds, like a comet with an extremely short interval.

We began to fear that he was going to self-destruct with a heart attack (or turn into a pool of butter), so we opened up the back door and on his next return trip he dashed into the yard and into his own house. And there he stayed, panting furiously.

As time went on, Sardo's visits became less frenetic, until he was actually walking around with an air of sanity. And he found a space behind a chair in the living room and made it his own private napping spot.

Eventually he began to spend as much time inside as out. He had full control over his schedule, barking at the back door to come in and doing the same when he wanted out. But he never spent the night inside. At 11:00 P.M. he would rouse himself from behind his chair, take a good long stretch, amble to the back door, and bark to go out for the night. Once out he'd take a look around to make sure the world was as he'd left it, then retire into his private residence.

His timing never varied by more than a few minutes. Maybe he'd announce his departure at 11:03, or maybe at 10:57. But he didn't miss by more than that. There was no way to explain his amazing punctuality. After all, he couldn't see the clock from behind the chair.

He even slept in his house during the dead of winter. Below-zero temperatures, blizzard conditions, he'd just curl up in the back of his house, snuggling in the blankets and hay we had put in. The colder it was, the better he seemed to like it. People who knew dogs guessed that he was part collie and part husky, and it must have been the latter that thrived in winter.

Then came a winter of record cold—it was reaching twenty-five below at night—and we didn't know if Sardo could withstand such temperatures, though he seemed perfectly willing to try. We held a family conference and decided to keep him in for a night. It wasn't easy. He barked to go out at his usual time, and we ignored him. He got angry and barked even louder.

We explained to him that it was for his own good, and then we all went to bed. He barked a few more times and then figured that if you can't beat them you might as well join them. He jumped onto my bed, walked over me in circles until he got it just right, and then collapsed with a sigh right over my legs.

He didn't spend another night outside for the rest of his life.

***

Sardo's relationships with other animals were stormy. Like any well-adjusted dog he chased cats, but only if they ran away from him first. If the cat just sat there instead of bolting, Sardo would go sniffing off in the other direction, as if he had more important things to do than terminating some mangy old cat.

He loved to chase birds, but always seemed puzzled that they could jump so much higher than he could. He ate ants, snapped at flies, and took stabbing nips at bees (with his lips curled away from his teeth to avoid stings).

One day he cornered a decent-size snake in the backyard. Before we could react, he grabbed the snake and started whipping it back and forth at high speed and then flinging it. Then he'd get behind it and do it again. We'd seen Lassie do this in the movies to save people, but we figured she had been trained. As far as we knew, Sardo had never had an acting lesson in his life.

Sardo was an unrepentant ladies' man. He loved female dogs without reservation, even when the relationship was strictly platonic. He did count some male dogs among his friends, but more often than not his attitude around other males was *You ignore me and I'll ignore you.*

He loved all human females, too, and was an absolute pussycat in the hands of any girl or woman. Men were more problematic—some he liked and some he didn't. But if a man was wearing boots, Sardo would attack his feet, biting at the boots and snarling. We didn't like to think about what had happened before we found him that might have caused this behavior.

***

Sardo sucked food up like a vacuum cleaner. If you had examined his feeding bowl after dinner with a high-powered electron microscope, you wouldn't have been able to find one molecule of food on it.

He ate almost everything, except medicine that he really needed. The vet showed us how to place a pill under his lower lip, hold his mouth closed, and stroke the underside of his jaw. This didn't work at all with Sardo. We could stroke until Judgment Day, but as soon as we let go of him he'd spit the pill right out.

Well, we reasoned, since he gulps his food down in a flash, the obvious thing to do is hide the pill in the middle of his favorite meal. So we made him scrambled eggs, stuck the pill in the middle, and put it in his bowl. We tried to appear casual about all this, so he wouldn't suspect we were trying to pull something shady on him. He ran to his bowl and inhaled the mess in an instant and then walked away.

We rushed over and looked down. There at the bottom of his immaculate bowl lay the little white pill. There wasn't a mark on it.

We tried the ruse with all his favorite foods, much to his delight, and the result was always the same: somehow the pill always ended up at the bottom of the bowl.

We finally found the one food that did the trick: Mallomars. A Mallomar was a cookie from heaven made of marshmallow and graham cracker layers. As big as they were, Sardo swallowed these without chewing. We pushed the pill into the marshmallow and smoothed it over. Sardo had to be wondering why, on this particular day, we were force-feeding him all his favorite foods, one after the other. But he wasn't about to look a gift horse in the mouth, even if it was a Trojan horse.

We tossed the tainted Mallomar to him; he caught it in the air and gulped it down. We waited for him to spit the pill out—we were expecting it—but it didn't happen. He had swallowed it hook, line, and Mallomar. Now he was begging for another one. But he was supposed to get only three pills a day, so he had to wait eight hours for the next one.

***

The human population seems to be quite equally divided between dog people and cat people. About every six months the magazine with our Sunday paper dutifully includes an article attributing different psychological profiles to these two groups. But I had an exchange once with a cat-owning friend that I think sums it up best.

"I'm a cat person. I don't like dogs," he stated.

"How can you not like dogs?" I asked. "You can have two-way communication with a dog. You can play games together. You can have a real relationship with a dog."

"Exactly," he barked.

Sardo's favorite game was hide-and-seek. He'd sit and stay in the living room on command, while I went and hid somewhere in the house. Then I'd scream, "Can't find me, Sard," and he'd run directly to my hiding spot and bark at me as though I were the biggest fool going.

I only managed to trick him once. I hid in the bathtub and drew the shower curtain closed. Twice he came into the bathroom, took a quick look around, and ran back out. Twice I yelled,

118

"Can't find me, Sard," and in this case he really couldn't. Finally he went to my mother and started to whine to her about it. She yelled to me to let Sard find me so as not to damage his doggy ego any further.

I yelled again and he came into the bathroom and stood there, bewildered. I made a noise and he banged the curtain back with his nose; there I was, lying in the tub, laughing like a loon.

He was extremely annoyed with me for stooping to such a low level to win a lousy game. Hiding in the laundry hamper was one thing. He could accept that. But as far as he was concerned, this bathtub ruse went beyond the bounds of fair play. I apologized to him and gave him a Mallomar as a peace offering.

We never could teach Sardo to run and hide himself. The concept of hiding in fun seemed to escape him. When Sardo hid, it was for real.

That first summer, we gave him his first bath. We dragged an old metal tub out of the shed and filled it with water. Then we picked Sardo up, put him in, and scrubbed him down. Like all kids, he hated it. When we were done, he jumped out and ran right for the grass, thrashing around in it like a maniac. He rolled over onto his back and kicked his rear legs, which sent him slithering through the grass like a snake. He rubbed his face in whatever dirt he could find.

When he was done, he needed a bath. Maybe that was the idea—maybe in the dog world that freshly bathed look just doesn't cut it.

Many months later it was time for another bath. Sardo was frolicking happily around the yard. We went into the shed and picked up the tub; as we did, it made a metal-tub kind of noise. By the time we came out of the shed Sardo was nowhere to be seen. He was hiding under a bush. This was serious business. This was no game.

On another occasion, during the early years when Sardo was still spending his nights outside, we were awakened by the sounds of someone tramping around on our roof. My father quickly dressed, grabbed a flashlight, and went outside to investigate. It turned out to be one of the local drunks, a harmless character, who was up there looking for something he thought he had lost. What more obvious place to look than on someone's roof? When he saw the flashlight he jumped to the ground and ran out the backyard. The police picked him up a few minutes later.

After the intruder had run off, we suddenly realized that we hadn't heard a word from our watchdog the whole time. Moreover, he was nowhere to be seen. Now we were really scared—could the drunk have hurt or even killed him?

We yelled for him. Nothing.

We ran out into the yard to look for him. He was there all right, hiding and trembling under the grapevine.

So there was no question that Sardo could hide very well when he wanted to. It was just that he wasn't about to waste his best efforts when it didn't really count. If we silly humans wanted to expend energy hiding for the pure fun of it, that was our problem. He'd save his for baths and drunks.

***

Sardo was afraid of any body of water larger than his drinking bowl. Rivers, streams, lakes, metal bathing tubs—they were all the same to him: he wanted no part of them. We wondered if he could swim if he had to. One day we got our answer.

Sometimes after work my father took Sardo golfing with him. To Sardo all those trees and all that green grass was canine Nirvana. He romped around ecstatically, always staying clear of my father's (perennially hurried) backswing.

On the third hole a pond separated the fairway from the green. In golf such an attractive feature of the landscape is called a "hazard." The name was especially appropriate on this particular day because Sardo got busy chasing a rabbit and, in the excitement, ran right over the edge of the fairway and into the drink. My father saw him disappear over the edge and then heard the splash. He dropped his clubs and ran over, prepared to jump in to save the drowning dog.

When my father arrived, Sardo was executing a very fine dog paddle in the middle of the pond, headed for the other side. When he had first landed in the water he was only inches from shore and could have turned right around and climbed out. But all he knew was that he had been only a whisker away from taking a bite out of that rabbit's ass when suddenly he found himself somewhere he absolutely didn't want to be, and by God he was going to head for the first land he saw. And that happened to be the other side of the pond. Luckily my father wasn't playing California's Pebble Beach, or Sardo would eventually have been adopted by some Japanese family and forced to spend the rest of his days wearing a flowery, doggy kimono.

He made it to the other side in fine shape, clambered up onto the muddy bank, shook himself off, and went about his business. My father was much relieved on two counts: he was still dry, and Sardo was still alive.

***

Like most dogs, Sardo loved to go for walks. Whenever he heard "C'mon Sard, let's go for a walk," he'd start barking wildly and run full speed to the door and bang off it with all fours. The only kind of weather he didn't like was rain (water again). If we opened the door for him and he saw it was raining, we'd pretty much have to coerce him to keep going. Once out he was as anxious to get back as we were.

We didn't use a leash to walk him—Catskill had no leash laws at that time and he was good about staying close and obeying commands. But sometimes he just got stubborn and decided that he wasn't ready to go home yet. This invariably occurred on the coldest evenings of the year, when it was twenty below with a forty-mile-per-hour wind. He seemed to become totally deaf at these times, because no matter how loudly we screamed for him, he remained totally oblivious to our existence. He would get very busy sniffing the scenery, as if he were in the process of figuring out some olfactory mathematical problem.

In one of my many attempts to map out Sardo's conceptual structure, I once shut myself up in my room with my portable tape recorder and taped about three minutes' worth of "C'mon, Sard, let's go for a walk." I really laid it on thick, too.

That evening he was napping behind his chair, and everyone was seated around the living room, eager to witness my ground-breaking research in animal psychology. I put the recorder on a chair, turned it on, and quietly left the room.

C'mon, Sard, let's go for a walk. C'mon, Sard.

He came bouncing out, ready to go for a walk with Denny, and ran over to the chair where the voice was coming from.

C'mon, Sard, let's go for a walk.

He sniffed warily at the recorder, and the rhythm of his tail-wagging began to break up. He looked around at the spectators, who were all trying to stifle hysterical laughter so as not to prejudice the experiment.

What Sardo knew was this. It was time for his walk. Denny was sitting in a chair telling him they were going for this walk. But Denny now had changed form into a plastic-smelling thing that had no legs or arms and didn't look as if it were about to walk anywhere. And everyone in the room was shaking and making weird sounds.

C'mon, Sard, let's go for a walk.

Sardo now realized that the laws of nature as he understood them had somehow been suspended, and he was not about to hang around any longer and play the fool. He moped back behind his chair and just stood there.

Now I was afraid that I had ruined him for life. I shut the recorder off and sat down in the same chair.

"C'mon, Sard, let's go for a walk," I said.

He didn't budge.

"Sardo, c'mon, let's go for a walk."

Still nothing. I started clapping my hands, stamping my feet.

"C'mon, Sard, let's go for a walk!" I yelled with all the excitement I could muster.

He stuck his nose out from behind the chair. After all, the Denny he had seen a few minutes earlier had no hands to clap or feet to stomp. So maybe things were getting straightened out here.

"C'mon, Sard, let's go for a walk."

He approached me uncertainly and sniffed. No more plastic smell! This was more like it.

Now Sardo was barking excitedly. He ran to the door and banged off it with all fours, and out we went.

The experiment had been a resounding success. I had proved beyond a shadow of a doubt that a human being can act like an idiot and that no self-respecting dog will put up with it.

***

René Descartes was a leading seventeenth-century French philosopher and mathematician. He was also a devout Catholic and a loyal adherent to the party line.

Catholicism teaches that only human beings have souls. These souls outlive the body and journey on to heaven or hell, depending on whether the human was naughty or nice. Animals, therefore, can't join us in the afterlife, though I've heard it rumored that they can go to purgatory, an eternal halfway house that is neither here nor there.

Descartes believed that the soul is the seat of consciousness; that is, when a human thinks, or has physical sensations, or experiences emotions, it is actually the soul, residing in the body, that is doing these things.

The implications of this for nonhuman animals are rather severe: they don't have thoughts, physical sensations, or emotions. (Many women would extend this description to men, as well.) Entities without consciousness, they are what Descartes referred to as "warm-blooded automatons": wonderful examples of God's ability to create, but nothing more than machines made of flesh and blood.

Some scientists of the day used Descartes's pronouncements as justification to perform vivisections, dissections of live animals, in order to observe the life processes as they were occurring. After all, if an animal screamed "in pain," this was no different really from a wagon wheel screeching on a cold morning.

I've often wondered if Descartes had a pet, a dog or cat perhaps. Did he talk to it, pet it, love it? The historical records don't tell us, but even if they did and he did, it wouldn't necessarily show inconsistency on his part. After all, a lot of men talk to their cars, pet them (we call it "waxing"), and love them.

To most of us now, Descartes's views seem primitive and incredible. Yet, the spirit (the soul, if you will) of Descartes's arguments underlies a lot of the feelings and actions of people toward animals today.

For a lot of people, animals are nothing more than pests to be eliminated, moving targets to be shot at, and food to be eaten. They are objects that sometimes foil us and sometimes serve us. The Cartesian viewpoint lives!

One of the common signs of a psychotic is the inability to relate to other people as thinking and feeling beings. What shall we call a person who is unable to relate to an animal as a thinking and feeling being? In fact, this phenomenon in children is often one of the first danger signs that the individual may be heading toward a similar attitude toward humans.

A creature that can solve a problem it has not been faced with before is a thinking being, and anyone with a dog or cat, for example, has seen it do this many times. A cat that figures out how to open a container it has never seen before, or a dog that hides the *second* time you try to bring it to the vet—these are examples of an active intelligence. And although we may not see such examples on an everyday basis, there is no reason to believe that the mental acuity which produces them is not ongoing.

When Sardo barked and jumped and ran in circles whenever we came home to him, can't we conclude that he was excited and happy? When he cowered and trembled, fearful? When he was accidentally kicked and he yelped, in pain?

Upon what reasonable basis could we deny these conclusions? The fact is, each one of us is very much an island. I know that I think and feel, but I have no direct proof that any other beings, even humans, do so. My evidence is purely circumstantial. I know how I act when I'm happy, or in pain, so when I see other humans acting similarly, I infer by analogy that they are happy or in pain. But I can never see their actual happiness or pain; we know that we are fooled sometimes—perhaps we are fooled all the time.

My belief that animals have a conscious life is also based on circumstantial evidence, but the evidence is just as strong. Animals are not inferior beings. They are just different.

Do unto others as you would have others do unto you.

Animals are others.

***

Sardo lived to the age of fourteen. He entered our lives when I was a kid and stayed until I was an adult. He chased around with me and my friends on the playground, he got to know my first girlfriend and others that followed (he loved them all), he trusted me to drive him around when I first got my license, he was there to greet me whenever I came home from college on vacation.

Finally it was time once again for me to leave for another school year. I packed my things as Sardo sadly watched. He knew very well what suitcases meant.

He lay down on the floor next to me as I petted him goodbye. He was old and suffering from the typical problems of a dog that age. I knew in my heart that it was probably the last time I would see him. I wondered if he knew that, too, because he never stayed still that long to get petted. He'd usually get antsy and go find something better to do. But not that day.

A few weeks later I called home and engaged in the normal small talk. I waited until the last moment to ask what was really on my mind.

"Is Sard still around?"

"No," my mother said.

"I didn't think so. I've got to go. I'll talk to you soon."

I sat down at my desk where a half-baked philosophy thesis was spread out and cried.

And I thought how, for the most part, life passes by in a smooth continuum, one stage gradually and imperceptibly becoming another, and you wonder how it was that you got to where you are. But then there are those times when you can literally feel part of your life breaking away, like a section of an iceberg cleaving off and sliding into the sea in a shock of noise and mist.

"No," my mother said.

7

First Jobs

One of the great milestones in life is the first time a nonfamily member pays you money for doing a job. It gives you the notion that you could quit grade school, pack your lunch pail, and move out on your own any time your parents made you mad enough. You could eat candy for supper, stay up as late as you wanted, and never have to take a bath.

Like many kids in the north, my first job was shoveling snow. In order to get those jobs my timing had to be perfect. If I went out while it was still snowing, nobody would hire me because they didn't want to have to pay someone again if it continued to snow. But if it stopped snowing and I didn't get out quickly enough, some other kid would get the job. The "good" houses, the ones that paid the best, wcrc well known, and all the kids headed for them first.

Planning my strategy was equivalent to making a tough investment decision. I could take the little house right next door, a sure thing, or pass it up in favor of one of the more distant and more lucrative ones. But if they were all taken by the time I got there, even if I rushed back, some kid would already be out front shoveling, taking the Milky Way right off my table.

Sometimes I would make all the wrong choices and end up with no jobs at all, and other times I would come home loaded with quarters, unable to lift my weary arms. The life of the itinerant snow shoveler was one of bust or boom.

Most jobs consisted of shoveling the sidewalk in front of the house. Sometimes a driveway was included—these paid more. The time and effort required depended on the type of snow. The light, fluffy kind was easy to pick up but tended to pour off the shovel as it was lifted. The wet, dense kind stayed on the shovel but was almost too heavy to pick up. Few sounds are as distinctive as that of a snow shovel scraping along a sidewalk on a cold winter day. The memory now makes me nostalgic and sick at the same time.

One winter my friend Freddy bequeathed me a shoveling job. For several years he had been the appointed snow shoveler for one of the good houses. Whenever it snowed the owners waited for Freddy to come—they wouldn't give the job to any of the other kids. It is hard to describe how envious we all were of this. Freddy didn't have to worry about timing his arrival just right. Whenever it snowed he could just sit there in his house, counting the quarters as they fell from the sky.

But this particular year Freddy decided to move up a rung on the ladder of capitalism and got himself a paper route. Unfortunately for Freddy, he soon found that on snow days he was unable to get all his papers delivered on time and also fulfill his shoveling duties. Because the paper route paid more and was steady work, Freddy made the practical, but still painful, decision: he told his client that he was retiring from the snow-shoveling business but that he had a friend who would take his place, if that was all right. And it was.

I was so excited. I truly loved Freddy for this. And I couldn't wait for it to snow.

It seemed like eons before we had another good snowstorm. I was afraid that the longer we went without snow, the more likely the owners were to forget the new arrangement and maybe line up someone else. Several times over the next few weeks it began to snow and I started getting psyched up, like an athlete before the big game. But then it would taper off and leave just a dusting on the ground, and I would be bitterly disappointed.

Finally we got a big one. It started snowing one evening and kept going all night and into the following day. School was cancelled. I couldn't believe how good life was getting. I kept watching out the window for it to stop, and as soon as it did I threw on my coat and boots, grabbed my shovel, and did my best to run through two feet of snow to my clients' house.

I knocked on the door and a very friendly lady came to greet me. I told her I was Freddy's friend, and she said she was glad I had come. She told me to do the walks and driveway, and then to knock on the door again when I was finished.

I set to work with verve, using all my skill and know-how to do the job perfectly. After ninety minutes of hard work, not a patch of ice was left on the driveway, not a trace of snow on the walk.

I knocked on the door again, slightly out of breath. The lady came out, surveyed my masterpiece, and told me I had done a wonderful job. I waited while she went and got some money.

Freddy had told me that the owners paid him according to how much snow there was and how long it took him. I would have been happy with a dollar. The lady came back to the door and counted out three dollars.

"Is that enough?" she asked.

"Yes," I choked.

"Okay, you come back the next time it snows, all right?"

"I will!"

I had hit the jackpot. I was rich. Three whole dollars! And I could do whatever I wanted with it. I didn't have to put it away for college or any of that nonsense.

I didn't trust carrying so much money in my pocket while I walked, so I shoved it into my mitten and held it tightly all the way home. During the journey I passed brigades of kids out looking for work, and I pitied them. *I used to be like them*, I thought.

For the next week I just floated through life. My real focus was on the next snowstorm, and this time it wasn't long in coming. Once again I arrived on my clients' doorstep minutes after the last snowflake fell.

A man came to the door.

"Hi, I'm the one who does your walks."

"Okay, when you're finished ring the bell."

I did another perfect job and then rang the bell. The man appeared again.

"Are you finished?"

"Yes."

"How much do I owe you?"

"Three dollars."

"Three dollars? Well, I'll tell you what—I'll give you the three dollars this time, but don't come back."

I didn't know what to say or how to explain that I would gladly do the job for one dollar and that the only reason I had said three was because, in fact, that's exactly how much the lady gave me the last time. Little kids are experts at making excuses to cover up for something they did wrong, but they're hopeless at sticking up for themselves when they're in the right.

He gave me the three dollars and closed the door.

I trudged back home crying bitter tears, my termination wages clutched tightly inside my mitten. I had lost my first job and I couldn't understand why. I was back in the ranks of the unemployed.

***

When I was eight years old, Grandpa Jake started to let me work the counter in his drugstore. I had hung around in there enough so that I knew where most of the popular nonprescription items were on the shelves, even though I had no idea what they were for. He taught me how to ring up sales on the big, cast-iron cash register that sat on the counter. He got a real charge standing hidden in the back of the store, watching the faces of the customers as a kid whose head barely cleared the counter asked if he could help them.

They told me what they wanted and I ran to the shelf to get it, often climbing on a stool to reach the item. Then I ran back, bagged it, rang it up, and made change.

Most people were good-natured about it. But sometimes men would act fidgety when I asked if I could help them, and they'd say they needed to speak to the druggist. Then Grandpa Jake would come over, and they'd ask for a box of "thingamajigs." The thingamajigs were in a drawer right under the counter. Jake would get a box, put it in a bag, and ring it up. I knew full well where they were and how much they cost, but for some reason neither Jake nor the men who came in to buy them seemed to want me dealing with them.

A number of times I asked Grandpa Jake what thingamajigs were. His answer was always the same.

"They're for men. You'll understand when you get older."

For a little kid who wanted to know everything about the world, this was not a satisfactory answer. After all, in school we were learning about atoms and solar systems, bacteria and mathematics. What could possibly be so difficult about thingamajigs?

My curiosity about thingamajigs grew until finally I couldn't stand it anymore. One day, when Grandpa Jake was out in front of the store talking to friends, I slipped a box of thingamajigs into my pocket. I tried to act casually for a few minutes, assuming that's what you're supposed to do after stealing something, and then I bolted out of the store and ran home as fast as I could.

I went out into the backyard and sat down behind a tree, and I opened the little box. I was nervous. Maybe thingamajigs were dangerous somehow. Inside was another little package covered in aluminum foil. I opened that, too. And there was the thingamajig. It was nothing but a long, greasy balloon.

What did grown men want with these things anyway? Why didn't they just go down to J. J. Newberry's and buy the colored ones?

So that was one mystery that remained unsolved.

There was another. Sometimes women acted embarrassed when I asked if I could help them, and they, too, would ask to speak to the druggist. But they didn't want thingamajigs. They wanted something called Kotex.

I knew right where these were, too. The boxes of Kotex were kept in the back of the store, and each one was covered in plain brown wrapping paper. Numerous times I asked Grandpa Jake what Kotex was for. His answer was always the same.

"They're for women. You'll understand when you get older."

I concluded that Kotex and thingamajigs must be related somehow: adults were reluctant to ask for them, they were kept hidden away out of sight, and I would understand when I got older.

I couldn't steal any Kotex because the boxes were too big. But one day fate intervened to provide me with a golden opportunity. A big carton of Kotex had been damaged in transit, and it now lay in the back room waiting to be reclaimed by the shipper. A corner of the box had been torn away and inside were some damaged smaller boxes.

I waited until Grandpa Jake went out to stand in front of the store. As soon as he did, I went into the back room and grabbed one of the small, crushed boxes of Kotex. I pried my finger into a small tear and made it large enough to see through. There was nothing but soft, white cloth in there. There was also printing on the box: FEMININE NAPKINS.

Napkins? What was so darned difficult to understand about that?

The only thing I could figure was that the man blew up his thingamajig, and then the woman wiped his face off with one of her feminine napkins.

***

When I was ten I worked as a pin boy at the bowling alley on Main Street. The bowling alley was like something out of a gangster movie: badly lit; replete with dingy, wooden furnishings; and permeated with the odor of stale cigar smoke. We kids loved it.

The owner was too cheap to pay minimum wage, so he hired underage kids like us to set the pins. We got fifteen cents a game, plus occasional tips from the bowlers.

To get to the staging area we walked down a narrow path between the last alley and the wall, and then opened a door into the area in back of the alleys. (In those days they were indeed called "alleys." This was before the bowling industry decided to market this filthy sport as "family entertainment" and began calling the alleys "lanes.")

In the back we ascended a platform, which ran behind the alleys. It was grimy and smelled of machines and old rubber. We got behind the alley we were attending and waited for the bowler to throw the first ball. The ball and whatever pins were knocked down ended up in the pit. We jumped down into the pit, picked up the ball, and rolled it down the ball return. Then we grabbed the fallen pins and placed them in the pin setter that hovered above the alley. But we had to make sure to place the pins in the correct slots.

We jumped back up on the platform and waited for the spare attempt. We jumped back down, returned the ball, and put the remaining downed pins in their slots. We then yanked on a rope, and the pin setter came down and placed the pins on their spots and then ascended back into position. (We all loved to set pins for groups that included women and children because they tended to throw lots of "pin boy's delights," or gutter balls.)

It sounds easy, but it was a real skill. If we placed a pin in the wrong slot in the machine, when the pin setter came down to start a new frame the misplaced pin would crash down on a pin still standing and the whole contraption would come to a grinding halt, skewed at an odd angle.

This was a rookie error, and when it was made the whole alley knew it. Then we had to ring the bell, and the mechanic on duty would come down and unjam the machine for our sorry ass while the bowlers drank their beer and yelled down that our mother should be helping us.

We also had to be careful of flying pins. It was common to get hit in the shins by one, and only pride kept away the tears. We could minimize the risk by moving farther back on the platform, but that meant that it took longer to jump back into the pit when the ball arrived. Each pin boy did a risk/benefit analysis and arrived at his own personal comfort zone.

It was important to be fast, because the bowlers liked this and would tip us more for it. The owner also liked it because he got more games per hour as a result. Rookies picked one pin up in each hand. Eventually most of us learned to pick up two in each hand.

Bobby Sulkey could pick up three in each hand. "Sulk" was a living legend, the king of the pin boys. He was older than the rest of us and had been doing it for years. He had several teeth missing and always had a cigarette stuck in one of the spaces. Sulk trained all the new boys, and we idolized him.

Doing one alley at a time was hard enough. When we got really good the boss would let us do two alleys at once, side by side. Now the challenge was doubled, as was the risk of being hit by flying pins. But we made twice as much money.

Sulk often did four alleys at once! He was a true artist. We often went down to the back just to watch him work. Like all great athletes, his speed seemed unhurried and effortless. He flowed from alley to alley, picking up six pins at once, tossing them into the correct slots in the pin setter with no hesitation (even when the spare left standing was some weird combination never before seen in bowling history), dodging flying pins without fear, guzzling Cokes, returning balls, yanking ropes, hopping from pit to pit, remembering if it was the first or second ball, dangling his cigarette.

Sulk never jammed a machine in his life.

Aside from setting pins, we had another important duty— avoiding the inspectors from the New York State Labor Department. Occasionally they came in to check for underage workers like us. When this happened the boss set off a secret buzzer in the back. As soon as we heard this alarm, we were to crawl out the one tiny window that had been put in the back wall for this very purpose.

Sulk had been through this drill so many times that he could literally dive through the window without touching the frame. Then he'd double back to Main Street and watch until the inspectors left, and then go right back in to finish his games.

I made big money in the bowling alley. One week I pocketed seven whole dollars. You couldn't beat that. But it finally all came to an end after the boss decided to hire a fat kid that nobody liked. He was hopeless. He kept on jamming the machine and could hardly drag himself back out of the pit after he jumped in. But the boss needed all the help he could get because the boarders were up and they loved to bowl—especially the Italians, who all had a bocci-like hitch in their strokes.

One afternoon the inspectors dropped in while the fat kid was working. The owner set off the buzzer. By the time the inspectors got down to the staging area we were long gone—except for the fat kid, who was stuck halfway through the little window with his butt still inside. The inspectors pulled him back in and found out he was eleven years old.

They shut down the business for a week, and that made an honest man of the owner. From then on he only hired kids sixteen or over, and he boarded up the little window.

Another promising career down the drain, strangled by government regulation.

***

It's astounding to think that up until the early 1900s, the everyday life of the average person had not changed significantly in thousands of years. Then, within a single lifetime, humans went from the horse and buggy to walking on the moon, from quill pens to e-mail, from the telegraph office to the cell phone.

To those of us who have lived through much of this transition, we each have our own personal moments of dislocation. At times, I still have to remind myself that the rich no longer drive cars costing $5,000. When I see a young woman with big breasts, it rarely enters my mind to wonder if they are manufactured. And I still go through an instant of wonder whenever I see someone talking on a telephone with no cord attached.

Yet, strange as it is to have lived through such transitions, I find it even stranger to think that the kids today have never known anything different. When my father used to tell Randy and me stories about his youth, there was nothing strange or novel about them (other than that he had grown up without TV, which did seem terrible). The same sorts of gadgets and machines that were common to our environment were part of our father's childhood as well.

The generation gap used to be a hairline crack. Now it's a chasm.

I don't have children of my own, having recognized long ago that I am psychologically unfit for that job (a realization that seems to escape far too many people before it's too late). But if I did, I can imagine trying to convince them that I grew up in a time when automatic pin setters and snowblowers didn't exist, and that I actually earned money doing what the machines now do.

Shortly after moving to Florida, I rented a house for which I was responsible for mowing the lawn. There was a power mower in the garage, but the Luddite in me has always hated them: they're noisy, smelly, and dangerous. (There's something about the sound of lawnmowers inundating suburban neighborhoods on weekends that makes me want to destroy civilization.)

I wanted a good, old-fashioned, powerless push mower, but trying to find one was like searching for a Gutenberg Bible. I was told by numerous store managers that they weren't made anymore. I just couldn't accept that progress had brought us to this point. Unless you have a very large lawn, a push mower is faster (you can run with it if you want to) and it is also great exercise—maybe that's why nobody in America wants one anymore.

While on a drive one afternoon, I came upon a rural, farm equipment store. I pulled in, certain that somewhere in a back corner was my lawnmower, covered with cobwebs and on sale since 1973. But even there the salesman laughed good-naturedly and said he hadn't seen one of those in quite a few years. But he pulled out a catalogue and found one, and I had him order it.

I loved it when it arrived. I loved the soft, self-generated whirring of the blade, and the feel of the grass being cut, reminiscent to me of the feel of the road through the steering wheel of a good sports car.

As I was racing around my front lawn with it one day, several neighborhood children on their bikes stopped and stared at me with strange expressions.

I said, "Hey, kids."

One of the boys piped up: "What are you doing, mister?"

I thought that it was my running with the lawnmower that had them puzzled.

"I'm mowing the lawn," I said.

"No, you're not," said one of the girls.

"Yes, I am. This is my lawnmower."

"No, it's not. It's not making any noise."

Then, of course, I realized what the problem was. These kids had never even imagined, let alone seen, a lawnmower without a motor.

"This is the way all lawnmowers used to be. It doesn't have a motor. You have to push it yourself and that makes the blade go around."

"Here, do you want to try it?" I offered.

The boy, obviously the bravest of the bunch, got off his bike and came over, and with great difficulty pushed the mower a few feet, while his friends giggled at the strange scene. Then they took off, probably to tell their parents about the weirdo down the street.

Most all of us, when we were kids, were familiar with some local character who wore old, out-of-fashion clothes, or talked to himself, or drove an antique car—someone who didn't fit in the world we were used to and who was to be given wide berth, just to be on the safe side.

As I watched the kids pedal off down the street, engaged in some animated conversation, I suspected that I had just applied for that role in our neighborhood.

***

At the age of twelve, I worked as a seasonal fruit picker. My season lasted exactly one day.

My friend John had heard that Lee Brown's Cherry Farm was hiring day laborers to pick cherries. The owner didn't care how old you were, and he paid an amazing fifty cents for each bucket picked. We figured we could each pick at least twenty buckets a day—that was ten whole dollars! We'd work there all summer and then we'd be rich. We'd quit school, buy a big boat, and cruise right down the Hudson River until we came to the South Sea Islands. We'd build a little house like we saw Robinson Crusoe do in the movies, eat coconuts and fruit, swing from vines, and just play all day long. There'd be nobody around to bug us.

Randy and I ran home to tell our parents and get their permission. (We didn't tell them the part about the South Sea Islands.) For some reason they didn't seem too excited about it.

They didn't believe that we'd make as much money as we thought.

That was the thing about our parents—they never believed anything. Our friend Ben told us that Frank Sinatra was his uncle and that he was coming for dinner that weekend and we could come, too, but when we excitedly told our parents did they believe it? Teddy told us that in the Pope's safe there was a note written by Jesus that gave the date of the end of the world, and that because this knowledge was so dangerous no one was given the combination to the safe except for the Pope. We ran home in terror to tell our parents. Did they believe that, either?

It was useless to tell them anything, just about.

But they gave us permission to work at Lee Brown's anyway, and early the next morning John, Randy, and I pedalled our bikes across the Rip Van Winkle Bridge to the other side of the Hudson, where Lee Brown's farm sprawled over hundreds of hilly acres overlooking the river. We rode down the farm road, surrounded by cherry trees sagging with fruit. We could have picked a bucket just by reaching out and grabbing cherries as we rode along. This was going to be criminally easy.

We got to the office and signed up for the day. There were a lot of coffee-colored people milling about, speaking some weird gibberish that couldn't possibly mean anything. We were introduced to our "super" and told that he would give us instructions. The super ordered us to follow him to the shed to get our ladders. We tagged along behind him like three little ducks on their first outing.

The shed contained a pile of ladders, each about a quarter-mile long. The super told us each to grab a ladder and then follow him into the orchard. I tried to pick one up and carry it on my hip like I saw the gibberish-speaking people doing, but I could only pick up one end at a time. John, who was bigger and stronger, had somehow managed to get both ends of his ladder off the ground at the same time and was actually starting to take a few weaving steps with it. Little Randy couldn't even drag his ladder off the pile and was fighting to choke back tears.

The super never even glanced back. He just kept walking into the orchard, carrying a set of buckets that looked like bathtubs with handles. We were all thinking the same thing—if we didn't get moving with those ladders, we were going to get fired before we had a chance to pick a single cherry. So I started dragging mine along the ground, and John ended up dragging both Randy's and his. It wasn't pretty, but we were managing to keep pace with the super.

But why wasn't he stopping already? We were walking down a dirt path with rows of trees all around, loaded with buckets of cherries. What was wrong with them? The super kept walking. Our arms were going dead, and with ever-increasing frequency we had to drop the ladders and rest for a few seconds. Then we'd pick them up and try to catch the super again. It began to remind me of the Bataan death march we had just seen in the movies.

Finally the super stopped. Whatever was so special about this particular spot was not apparent, since it looked exactly like every other part of the orchard we had just suffered through.

"Okay, you guys start on this tree here. You fill these buckets brimmin' full. Every so often I'll come by'n the truck to pick up your buckets and credit you for 'em. You pick this tree clean, and then you can start on this other'n here."

And with that he was gone, leaving us totally alone in a sea of cherry trees, with nothing but our giant buckets and ladders.

We each grabbed a bucket and started picking the cherries off the bottom branches of our tree. We could do this from the ground, and in only a few minutes our buckets were half full. It was as easy as we had thought. We were going to make tons of money at this. As usual, our dumb parents were wrong again.

Soon we had picked all the cherries from the bottom branches and could reach no more of them even standing on our tiptoes.

It was time for the ladders. John and I grabbed one and together managed to stand it on end. But we weren't strong enough to control it very well, and it crashed into the tree. It snapped off a few smaller branches and came to rest at an odd, unclimbable angle.

We pushed and pulled at the ladder to reposition it, in the process knocking off some cherries that Randy quickly retrieved and put in *his* bucket. Finally we stabilized the ladder, and John climbed up a few feet and started picking the cherries at the next level. He had to haul his bucket up and hang it on a hook on the ladder next to where he was standing. It was easy pickings for a few minutes, but then he had to reach, and then climb a little higher, and so it went. And for all that, the level of cherries in his bucket didn't seem to change at all.

We tried to put a second ladder up on the other side of the tree and had just as much trouble as before. We finally positioned it, and I nearly pulled my arms out of my shoulders trying to haul my bucket up the ladder. At each level, as the cherries got farther out of reach, the limits of personal courage were tested as we leaned farther and farther out to grab a few cherries dangling here and there.

The sun got higher, the temperature got hotter, and now some kind of flea was attacking us in swarms. Our hands and arms were badly scratched from banging against the branches and twigs, and we'd eaten enough cherries ourselves that we each could have puked up a bucket's worth.

After a couple of hours, we had filled up three buckets. We were dead tired, but we were proud. Our first buckets! Wait'll the super sees this! Where was that damned truck anyway? We wanted our credit.

Back up the ladders we went. Randy's job had become that of picking up cherries that we threw down to him. That way we didn't have to keep hauling our buckets higher and higher up the ladders.

Finally we saw a truck coming down the path, trailing a cloud of dust. It stopped next to our tree and the super jumped out.

"How you boys doin'?"

"We got three buckets and we're working on the next three."

He came closer and looked at our buckets.

"These ain't filled up enough. These are level buckets. You got to fill 'em brimmin' full. They's got to be a mound of cherries on top, like these ones here."

He pointed to the buckets in the back of his truck. Each one was crowned by a mountain of cherries that went several inches higher than the top of the bucket. They was brimmin' full.

He got back in the truck and drove away. We ran into the orchard to avoid the dust tornado kicked up by the truck. We were discouraged. It had taken us so long to fill the last few inches of those buckets, and still we weren't done.

Back to the ladders—another hour of death-defying aerial maneuvers to put those little mountains on top of our buckets.

We finally got to the point where we just couldn't reach any more of the cherries on our tree. There were still some there, but they were either too high or too far out on thin branches for us to reach them. We had done all we could do with that tree. And the super had said that when we finished with this tree, we could start on the next one.

So we moved over to the adjacent tree and life was good again. With all those cherries on the bottom branches, our second buckets began to fill rapidly. But soon enough we were forced to struggle with the ladders again.

Then we had an idea. While John and I were toiling away on the ladders, Randy could start picking the bottom cherries off the next tree. That way we were packing in more labor per unit time. Efficiency was very important in the workplace.

The afternoon wore on and we wore out. By the end of the day we had managed to fill nine buckets brimmin' full. We were lying in the grass when the truck pulled up for the final pickup.

The super jumped out and came over to us.

"Let's see how you did."

He checked out our nine buckets and grunted. Then he walked over and inspected our tree.

"Hey, I thought I told you not to start on no other tree until you finished with the first one?"

"We just couldn't reach any higher on that one."

"And then you started on this tree here, and grounded two other ones. When the hell were you plannin' on finishin' these other ones?"

"When we come back tomorrow?" I said tentatively.

"There ain't gonna be no tomorrow for you boys. You bring the ladders back to the shed, and I'll pay you for these buckets. Then you get out of here and don't come back no more."

He drove off and again the dust chased us into the orchard.

Exhausted, we slowly dragged our ladders back up the road. As we neared the shed we saw dozens of the tan guys streaming out of the orchard, carrying their ladders under their arms like the morning newspaper, laughing and pretending to talk in their nonsense language.

The super was sitting at a table, hunched over a little box of money. We lined up with the tan guys to get paid. We couldn't believe what we were hearing. As each one in line got to the super he identified himself, and then the super would look down his list and call out:

"Gomez, fifteen buckets, seven dollars and fifty cents."

"Sandoval, nineteen buckets, nine dollars and fifty cents."

How was that possible? These guys must have chopped the trees down and then picked the cherries.

Now it was my turn in front of the super.

"Three buckets, a dollar fifty."

The same for Randy and John.

We trudged over to our bikes and had a hard time getting our legs over the crossbars, we were so beat. Luckily the orchard road was downhill, so we coasted all the way back down to the main road. Nobody said much.

Then we had to pedal our bikes back over the bridge, directly into the teeth of a river breeze stiff enough to blow us backwards if we stopped pedalling.

Finally we made it across the river and back to the familiar tree-lined streets of Catskill. We were each thinking the same thing: no boat, no South Sea Islands, no swinging on vines, no nothing. Somehow our parents had been right on this one, and that made us feel even worse. Now we'd have to endure that "someday you'll learn to listen to us" look that they got at times like this.

"Fuck the super," said Randy.

"Yeah, fuck that super," John and I echoed, flipping very vigorous birds in the direction of Lee Brown's Cherry Farm.

***

Years later, when I was in high school, I got my first legitimate summer job. I had wanted one long before then—all my friends had been working during the summers for years—but my father always discouraged it.

"Enjoy being a kid while you can," he said. "Soon enough you'll be working for the rest of your life. Don't rush it."

And it is odd how kids want to work just like they see the grown-ups doing. They don't know any better yet. Think of all the runts in the world pushing little toy lawnmowers around. In only a few years they won't go near the genuine article without death threats.

I didn't know any better yet, either, so I finally convinced my father to let me enter the work force. And by hook or by crook (both actually, in the guise of political patronage), I landed a job working for the New York State Regents Department in Albany, thirty miles up the river from Catskill.

I found a local man who took riders up and back each day for a small weekly fee. His name was Ernie and he was a career

auto mechanic with the state. Ernie was a cynical, irascible, sar-
castic old coot, and I loved him. He made me laugh so hard on
the way to work each morning that I always arrived hoarse. My
voice cleared up during the day (there wasn't that much to laugh
about at work), and then I got hoarse again on the way home.
The three strait-laced women who rode with us didn't seem to
find him funny at all. This made it even better.

Ernie had two main topics of discourse: politicians and mar-
riage. His views on the former were summed up in his conten-
tion that all the criminals should be let out of jail and replaced
with the politicians, so that the world would be a safer place.

As for matrimony, whenever we got behind a car with a
couple sitting close together in the front seat, Ernie would triumphantly announce, "They're not married."

Ernie was the kind of driver who honked at people who let a
little thing like a red light stop them. One morning on the way
to work he did that to the car in front of us, and a big, mean-
looking character got out of the car and started walking toward
us. He did not look like the type to let a mere car window (which
Ernie was rolling up furiously) interfere with his goals in life.

I saw it all coming. He was going to punch out our window,
drag Ernie into the street, and beat him silly. And I was going to
have no choice. As the only other male in the car, puny though I
was, I would have to make the futile gesture of defending Ernie
so that I could get beaten silly myself.

But Ernie saved the day for both of us. He backed the car up
and then pulled right over a lawn to get around the would-be
assassin, leaving him screaming and gesturing wildly, but harm-
lessly.

That cured Ernie of his nasty little habit. He did not honk
his horn at anyone at a red light for over a week.

The Regents Department was responsible for the New York
State Regents exams in various subjects that were given to high
school students. The purpose of these standardized tests was to

ensure that illiteracy and ignorance were equitably distributed over all school districts, and not restricted to just a select few.

The Regents Department created the exams and distributed them to all the high schools in the state for administering at the end of the school year in June. Then, after the teachers corrected the exams, they were all sent back to the office where I worked. My job, along with a few other summer workers, was to count the exams, collate them, bundle them, and store them. We weren't supposed to read them.

We read them every chance we got. The most fun to read were the ones with failing grades. These were very easy to find. The exams in nonmathematical subjects consisted of essays and multiple-choice questions. What impressed me most that summer was how stupid people can mock the law of averages.

Consider a set of forty multiple-choice questions, each having four choices. The law of averages dictates that if you choose answers at random, on average you'll get ten right. You don't have to know anything about the subject; you don't even have to read the questions. All you have to do is just pick any forty answers at all. Or, sit a monkey down with a pencil and let him do it. The law of averages is on your side (or the monkey's).

Stupid people, however, only get three or four right out of forty. They never get ten. They never even get five. Three or four, that's it.

This is cause for wonder. After all, these test takers are human beings, presumably the most intelligent animal in the universe. They attend classes and are at least semiconscious part of the time. And even if everything the teacher says goes in one ear and out the other, it would be reasonable to expect that a few synapses would retain at least a trace memory of the journey—enough to outdo the monkey, in any case, who has been cutting classes his entire simian existence.

But it doesn't happen that way. These people are the fun house image of idiot savants: whereas the idiot savant has limited areas of brilliance beyond scientific explanation, the just plain stupid person has areas of witlessness beyond mathematical probability.

So we perused the exams and marvelled at the future of America. Then we bundled them up and stored them. The storage room was three floors up from our office, and the actual process of storing the exams had to be performed twice a week. Two people stacked a large cart with bundled exams, walked the cart down the hall to the elevator, took the elevator up three floors, rolled the cart to the storage room, placed the bundles on the appropriate shelves (sometimes using a ladder), and then returned.

There were six of us summer workers and we alternated going to the storage room. To break the monotony, we decided to turn the storage routine into a race. Time was kept from the moment the cart left the office to the moment it returned, and was recorded along with the names of the team members. At the end of the summer, the winning team was to be treated to lunch by the two losing teams.

But this competition had a twist. In the spirit of government workers everywhere, the winning team was to be the one that took the longest. Our contest had only one rule, and we all were on the honor system to obey it: when going on a storage run, both team members had to keep moving at all times, however slowly, and the movement had to be directly contributory to the task at hand.

Performed at normal human speed, the storage run could have been made in thirty minutes. (This was a theoretical estimate only, since normal human speed has never been attained by anyone in a government office building.)

Our initial runs took about an hour, but as the weeks passed and we got better, we began threatening the ninety-minute barrier. Finally, on one of the last runs of the summer, my partner Neil and I put forth what can only be described as a Zen-like effort to come in at one hour and forty-two minutes flat. We won the lunch handily and were very happy.

By mid-July all the Regents exams from around the state had been safely tucked away in the storage room. That marked the beginning of our next big project: packaging the Regents College Scholarship exams for distribution. This exam was administered once a year to all high school seniors around the state, and the top scorers in each county were awarded tuition grants of various magnitudes to attend New York State colleges. It was a big deal.

Several hundred thousand exams awaited distribution, each with a serial number printed on it. Our job was to take an exam, put it into the envelope with the corresponding serial number, and then secure the flap of the envelope with a little blue seal that we wet with a sponge.

During this period our office became a highly secured area. A guard checked the clearance of anyone trying to enter, and each night all the exams were locked away in a huge safe. If even one copy found its way out of that room, it would compromise the integrity of the whole exam. A few years earlier an exam did disappear, and it became a major crisis involving top state officials and investigators. Security was heightened even more as a result of that episode.

Just as with the Regents exams, we were instructed not to read the scholarship exams as we handled them, and we were also required to sign an oath that we would not divulge any of the contents.

Because a student who did well on the exam could win thousands of dollars' worth of scholarships, it was to be expected that some unscrupulous people would offer to pay quite handsomely for a sneak preview of the exam questions. In fact, I was appalled when the son of a rich family in Catskill had the audacity to offer me $200 for information about the upcoming exam. My family had always prided itself on its reputation for honesty and integrity. He should have known that I would never compromise that in any manner for less than $500.

Upon arriving at work in the morning, each one of us was given a pile of exams and a stack of correspondingly numbered envelopes, a container of blue seals, and a wet sponge. Our quota was to pack 1,000 exams per day each, which worked out to about two exams per minute for an eight-hour day. We had to work pretty steadily to hit that number, which left little time to slack off. Because the exams were numbered sequentially, Mary, our supervisor, could tell exactly how many we had done at the end of the day by checking the beginning and ending serial numbers.

So there the six of us sat, day after day, stuffing and sealing. After a week of this my sleep patterns were totally disturbed. Instead of restful sleep I'd fall into one of those sickening semideliriums where you're trapped doing the same thing over and over, and you want to stop but you can't. In this case it was stuffing and sealing envelopes.

By the end of the second week Neil and I were straddling the borderline of psychosis. We talked about quitting. We couldn't imagine doing this for one more day, let alone the rest of the summer.

Out of this desperation came a brilliant idea. Instead of fighting the task, we would embrace it. We would become the all-time greats of stuffing and sealing. Racing against the clock in a cooperative effort, the challenge was to see how many exams we could pack in one hour.

We returned to the task with anticipation and excitement. Now we had something to shoot for. For the rest of the day we experimented with different techniques, and we found that Henry Ford had been right: specialization of labor is the most efficient means of production. I became the stuffer and Neil the sealer.

Before each hour-long trial began, we'd set up. We piled all the exams and envelopes on my side of the table, the seals and sponge on Neil's side. I'd put a few hundred envelopes in my lap, with the corresponding exams stacked near the edge of the table. Neil would wet a bunch of seals and stick them up and down his arms for quick access.

At the beginning of the hour we were off. I'd flick the top exam off the table and guide it on the fly into the envelope I held open in my lap, then toss the envelope across the table to Neil. He'd quickly check that the serial numbers matched, then rip a seal off his arm and slap it on the envelope flap.

We moved at blinding speed for the entire hour. We also developed an assortment of tricks to bump up the output even more. We found that the sealing went slightly faster than the stuffing, so any time Neil got ahead of me he would prewet more seals, or even stuff some exams himself. The idea was for each of us to be productive every second of that hour.

After a few days of practice, we were ready for the ultimate all-out effort. We were going for our own world record. I had trouble getting to sleep the night before because I knew we were about to make history.

The next day we nervously set up our assembly line. The other workers paid us little attention, having long before concluded that we were wacko.

Neil hit his stopwatch and for a solid sixty minutes we moved like a well-oiled, precision machine. It was beautiful! At the end of the hour we slumped down on the table, arms aching and trembling with the effort. And then we checked the ending serial number. We had packaged 1128 exams in one hour! One every 3.2 seconds!

For the rest of the morning we stuffed and sealed at a leisurely pace, joking and laughing and just generally revelling in our accomplishment. Mary glanced at us several times from her desk in the corner of the office, but remained silent. By lunch we had packed over 2,000 exams, our combined quota for the day.

After lunch, we once again sat there having an all-around good time, packing an exam at random intervals. Mary glared at us several times but still said nothing. She obviously was biding her time until the end of the day, when she would catch us far below our quota and give us hell.

A few minutes before quitting time we started packing up, and Mary headed straight for us. She checked the serial numbers and looked clearly disappointed when she saw that we each had surpassed our quota. What could she say, except "See you tomorrow"? We had her right where we wanted her. We had beaten the system. We could now finish our daily quota in a matter of a few hours, and then spend the rest of the day enjoying ourselves.

The next morning we again finished our quota before lunch, and then spent some time practicing our rubber band shooting technique. (I was extremely good at this, having once demonstrated my skill at a party by snuffing out a candle from across the room. Unfortunately, everyone there was too stoned to recognize that this was not the normal way to put out a candle.)

Mary was watching us like a vulture and, of course, we wouldn't have wanted it any other way. After lunch we didn't even make a pretense of doing any useful work. Why should we? The powers that be had calculated that 1,000 exams were a good day's work, and we were giving them that. So what if it only took us two hours? That's what America was all about—finding a better way to do things, right?

Mary was acting nervous. It didn't look like she was getting any of her own work done now. Finally she yelled over to us.

"Hey, boys, if you don't get to work, you're not going to make your quota."

"It's already done," I yelled back. The other workers were trying unsuccessfully to keep a straight face, bearing witness as they were to an exciting new wrinkle in the classic struggle between labor and management.

"Well, let's see about that," she said, as she rose from her desk and approached our moribund assembly line.

"So it is," she said as she checked the serial numbers. Her authoritarian tone had lost its usual punch.

She returned to her desk and said nothing more to us for the rest of the afternoon. We continued to chat and have a grand old time, every few minutes going through the formality of stuffing and sealing another exam as a complimentary bonus to the State of New York. We had taken on the bureaucracy and beaten it at its own game. We knew we were destined to become legends among government workers everywhere.

The next day, as usual, we had gotten our quota done before lunch and had geared the assembly line down to idle. Mary sauntered over and asked, "You boys got your quotas for the day?"

"Yes, we sure do."

"Well, I've talked it over with my supervisor, and we've decided that since you boys do such a good job and can pack these exams so much quicker than anyone else, it's only fair that, starting tomorrow, we raise the quota for each of you to 2,000 a day."

Her tone had regained its full vigor, and she triumphantly sashayed her way back to her desk.

Neil and I sat there stunned. We hadn't beaten shit. They had another move that we never even suspected. They probably always would.

We had learned a valuable lesson for the workplace and for life in general. Once you put the spotlight on yourself, don't expect to be able to slip back into the shadows. Today's heroic achievement becomes tomorrow's minimal requirement.

***

Toward the end of the summer, we came to work one morning to find several workmen in the next room assembling a big machine. It had conveyor belts, pulleys, and gears, and it took up most of the room—it looked serious.

"What's it for?" I asked.

"It's going to automate the packaging of the Scholarship Exams," we were told.

Neil and I looked at each other in wonder—apparently we had shaken up the bureaucracy so badly that now they wanted to replace us with a machine.

I quickly cut to the chase.

"How many exams can it pack in an hour?"

"Thousands."

These guys had to be joking with us; the machine had to be for some other purpose. Why would the state pay probably $100,000 for a machine just to take the place of a handful of minimum-wage coolies? (Remember, I was very young when I wondered this.)

We went and asked Mary if what we had been told was true, and she confirmed that it was.

Neil and I were distraught. Yes, we had hated the job of packaging the exams, but we had turned the situation around so that it had become a source of status for us. Now they were going to take it away from us.

We decided that we weren't going to surrender peacefully. Like John Henry, we were going to go down swinging (or, in this case, stuffing and sealing).

We issued a challenge to the machine operators: a one-hour race against Neil and me.

We told Mary, who seemed to like the idea. (She undoubtedly felt we would be humiliated by the heartless beast next door and was looking forward to it.) We bragged about the event to our co-workers. Word got around and soon people that we didn't even know started greeting us in the halls and asking when the big match was to take place.

We hoped it was soon because we were primed to go, but there was one problem. In testing, the operators could not get the machine to run more than a few minutes before it ate up a (dummy) exam and came to a shrieking halt. Then it took an hour for them to disassemble part of the belt mechanism, clean the paper shreds out of it, and put it all back together again.

Day after day, as Neil and I coolly and efficiently packaged the exams by the thousands, keeping ourselves in peak condition, the noises emanating from the next room became quite predictable: the clunk-clunk sound of the machine processing exams, then after a few minutes the high-pitched squeal of rubber and steel being tortured, then silence, followed by increasingly creative profanity concerts. An hour or so later, it would all begin again.

I wish I could describe in detail how, in the final confrontation, Neil and I beat the machine and struck a blow for humanity. But I can't, because the summer ended and they still hadn't gotten the machine to work for more than a few minutes at a time. This was without a doubt one of the biggest letdowns of my young life.

Neil and I, who were prone to philosophical analysis even then, had some serious discussions about whether or not we could truthfully say that we had beaten the machine. Neil argued that, in effect, we had beaten the machine in numerous hour-long trials: every time the machine started up it signalled the beginning of a race. Then when it broke soon after while we continued to work for the hour, we packaged more exams and so won that particular competition.

If that line of reasoning didn't persuade me, Neil had another. What was the point of racing the machine anyway? he asked. It was to see who (or what) was the better exam packager. The machine never even got good enough to *challenge* us. Therefore, though the "official" race never occurred, the truth it was intended to reveal was clear: we were the better packager.

What was even clearer than that, however, was that Neil should have become a Presidential press secretary (instead of a dentist—go figure).

The world is too enamored of machines. It's gotten to the point where people want machines to do everything for them, and the technology wizards are scrambling to oblige.

In my youth, bragging rights were founded on personal attributes:

I'm faster, more powerful, smarter than you.

Nowadays the loci of status have shifted:

My machines are faster, more powerful, smarter than yours.

The funniest cartoon I ever saw in my life was a Tom and Jerry episode circa 1968. The setting of the cartoon was "Sometime in the Future." Tom (the cat) no longer chased Jerry (the mouse) around; and Jerry no longer constructed elaborate ruses to crush, burn, and blow up Tom.

Instead, Tom sat at a console in the comfort of his home and at long distance controlled a robot Tom; and Jerry sat at a similar console in his house and controlled a robot Jerry. Now, it was the robot Tom who chased the robot Jerry around, and it was the robot Jerry who constructed elaborate ruses to crush, burn, and blow up robot Tom.

Life at one remove. Sometime in the future.

***

The following summer I was lucky enough to land a real plum job: park ranger at North Lake State Park up in the mountains. My job consisted of riding a motor scooter around all day, aiding visitors, directing traffic, and looking out for violations like dogs (which were not allowed in the park) and unauthorized camping. I also took it upon myself to keep an eye on the girls at the beach.

Ross, the park manager, was an old curmudgeon who lived by himself in a log cabin on the grounds. He didn't seem to like anybody and he made no exception of me. My first day he gruffly showed me how to operate the scooter, gave me my badge and uniform, told me my duties, and then disappeared back into his cabin.

The park covered a large area and I put 100 miles on the scooter that first day. I found, however, that the scooter had a minor quirk: the brakes would sometimes lock and nearly throw me over the handlebars. The fact that this was dangerous didn't bother me nearly as much as the fact that it detracted from the panache of my arrivals at the beach.

The next morning I reported the problem to Ross, but he was unimpressed.

"There's nothing wrong with the scooter. You just need to learn how to ride it."

What I learned to do was avoid using the brakes at all and just drag my feet to slow down and stop. This was hard on my sneakers, but easier on my image.

Dogs in the park seemed to be Ross's fondest obsession. One afternoon as I was putting the scooter away for the day, Ross came out of his cabin and started to yell at me because he had heard that someone had seen a dog near the beach sometime that afternoon. He wanted to know why I hadn't done anything about it.

"Ross, I was over at the beach several times this afternoon and I didn't see any dog there."

"Well, someone told me there was."

"Ross, it's possible that there was a dog there when I wasn't, but I can only be in one place at one time. This is a big park. All I can tell you is that I haven't seen any dogs around here all day."

At that very moment, three dogs came bounding out of the woods and cavorted down the road right by us. Ross pirouetted on his heel, went into his cabin, and slammed the door so hard it scared the poor dogs.

***

I had been on the job only two weeks when the scooter refused to start. When I reported this to Ross, he uttered some sort of primitive noise I took to mean "you dumb ass" and he marched to the shed to start it himself. I watched in quiet euphoria as he wore himself out trying to kick-start the scooter, and I was slightly disappointed when he didn't suffer an infarction.

Ross then reported to me that the scooter had suffered this problem several times over the years, and it had to be sent out for repair. But this time Ross decided that the scooter wasn't going to be sent out again, and he wasn't about to buy a new one.

"So how do I get around the park?" I asked.

"Walk."

"Ross, I put 100 miles a day on that thing doing my job."

"Do the best you can."

I did just that. The next day I brought a paperback book with me and stuffed it into my pack. I started walking along the road to the beach. Ross's habits were well known to all of us—first thing in the morning he toured the park in his truck, then went back into his cabin. He usually wasn't seen again until late afternoon, when he took another tour.

Ross came by in his truck, and I gave him a big wave. As soon as the truck was out of sight, I walked into the woods, found a cozy spot against a log, and spent a pleasant morning reading. I came out for lunch, then went back to my hideaway for the rest of the afternoon. Late in the day I hit the road again in time to be seen by Ross on his final tour of the day.

I got a lot of reading done that summer.

One afternoon the stress of the job started getting to me and I needed to take a nap. I went deeper into the woods, found a cool spot under a bush, and went to sleep. I began to have a strange dream in which a little girl kept screaming, "Mommy, Mommy, look—the park ranger is dead!"

I opened up my eyes and saw the girl of my dreams standing next to the bush. I sat up and the frightened little girl ran back to her rather large family, all of whom were staring at me in wonderment from a main hiking trail I had neglected to notice.

"Looks like my break is over, " I said as I stood up, brushing leaves and twigs off my spiffy uniform.

The family seemed very uncertain about all this, and they resumed hiking at what seemed to be a very ambitious pace. I would have thought that coming across a ranger like that in the middle of the woods would have made them feel safer, but there's no figuring some people.

***

I rode up the mountain and back each day with another worker who was on the maintenance crew. His was the kind of job that was dirty but somebody had to do: emptying the trash receptacles, cleaning the bathhouses and bathrooms, picking up trash from the grounds. And every Wednesday he and his crew had to drive around the park with the "honey wagon" and pump out the latrines. The first Wednesday that I rode back down the mountain with him I literally had to hang my head out the window the whole way like a dog. After burning the clothes I wore that day, I resolved to take my own car to work on Wednesdays for the rest of the summer.

The maintenance crew had their own initiation rite for rookies. In the back of each latrine, there was a pit that was protected by a locked cover. At the top of the pit was a pipe, controlled by a valve. To empty the latrine, the crew opened the cover, reached down, and opened the valve. The raw sewage rushed out into the pit, where it was vacuumed up by the honey wagon.

A new guy on his very first honey wagon detail was instructed to get into the pit to turn the valve on, because (he was told) it was the only angle from which the valve could be turned, and (he was told) the sewage took about thirty seconds to start flowing, plenty of time to get back out of the pit before anything hit the fan.

The subsequent reactions to the baptisms ranged from hilarity to murderous rage. (Mostly the latter.)

Now, after a lifetime of various work experiences, I can assure you of one thing: sooner or later, no matter who you are or what your job or career, it's your turn in the pit.

8

School

The first big shock in a child's life is delivered when he or she is expelled from the comforting confines of the womb into the open-air world of ultimate freedom. The next big shock arrives five years later when the child gets pushed back into a musty-smelling enclosure called "school."

I didn't like school at all. For one thing, it forced me into contact with aliens—kids from other neighborhoods. I didn't like these kids because they seemed different in a way I couldn't quite put my finger on. And for the first time in my life I was forced to share breathing space with girls who weren't relatives.

The curriculum in elementary school consisted of four Big Deals: learning to read, learning what kinds of things you had to do to a bunch of apples to get a different bunch of apples, learning that the earth goes around the sun, and learning to look at a globe and figure out where America was. If we managed to learn these things in the first few years we were doomed to terminal boredom, because they insisted on teaching them to us again and again every year right on up through the sixth grade.

Elementary school was a minefield of snot. It was everywhere, especially under desks and chairs. We quickly learned not to put our fingers anywhere we couldn't see, or we would undoubtedly make contact with a crusty, hard nodule. That's if we were lucky. If we weren't so lucky the nodule wouldn't be so hard or so crusty, and if it absolutely wasn't our day it would stick to our fingers.

Irving School was a three-story, brick building with an old wooden interior, and like schools everywhere it smelled of floor wax, disinfectant, and chalk. It was almost certainly a horrible firetrap. Occasionally we had unannounced fire drills, to prepare us for unannounced fires. The bell would go off in the middle of class and the teacher would shepherd us into nice straight lines and march us down the fire escape. Talking or laughing was strictly forbidden, as this presumably would have made a real fire burn faster.

We also had atomic bomb drills. When the nuclear-war siren went off (it sounded distinctly different from the fire bell), we scrambled underneath our desks, put our butts in the air, and buried our heads in our arms. If we guys had been old enough to appreciate girls, this would have been a worthwhile exercise, but as it was it all went to waste.

It's strange now to recall that nobody seemed to question the rationality of hunkering down under furniture while the world melted down around us. But that was during a time when the government had convinced Americans that if a nuclear attack should occur, all we had to do was close our windows and blinds and eat canned goods for a week, and then come out and clean up our lawns.

We boys in elementary school always rode the ragged edge of getting in trouble, because almost every operative instinct pushed us toward behavior that the teacher inevitably found unacceptable. We wanted to talk to our friends sitting next to us. We needed to put our heads down on our desks and take siestas. We had sudden urges to shoot rubber bands at the heads of the girls sitting in front of us. We wanted to scream, to laugh, to call the teacher an asshole right in front of everybody and go out in style.

But we forced ourselves to sit there in those hard little hiney-fitting wooden chairs and be "well-behaved." Until one of the instincts just got too strong and refused to be denied.

The lowest level of punishment was a verbal reprimand. This was totally ineffective because it didn't hurt one bit and it made all our friends laugh.

The next level was a stretch in the coat room. This wasn't so bad, either, because we could walk around in there all we wanted and give the teacher the finger. It was totally without risk (unless we weren't watching the door), and it was genuinely therapeutic.

The highest level, and the one that was universally feared, was having to go see Mrs. Avery. Mrs. Avery was the school principal, a white-haired, physically imposing lady of unknown age and relentlessly stern demeanor. Mrs. Avery's office was on the third floor, and what went on behind her huge wooden door was the stuff of playground legend.

Even the hardest of hard cases—the ones defiant enough to retain their smirks as they were marched up that well-worn stairway on their way to see Mrs. Avery—were often seen blubbering shamelessly on the way down.

Whether Mrs. Avery actually ever hit anyone with that leather strap she was reputed to keep in her desk is hard to say. Unfortunates who had taken that long march up to her office would say things like "she almost hit me" or "she sort of hit me." Probably the sheer terror of facing Mrs. Avery in her lair was worse than any corporal punishment she might have meted out.

In retrospect, the whole Mrs. Avery aura was probably a very well-constructed artifice that had developed over the years as an effective way to control behavior. The teachers played it to the hilt, acting like reluctant, duty-bound executioners whenever they threatened us with going to see Mrs. Avery.

In fact, Mrs. Avery may well have been the scholastic counterpart of the mummified matriarch of Bate's Motel.

***

In elementary school I was a horrible know-it-all. I loved to read and because of that I did it well (or vice versa). I became a little knowledge sponge. I was neurotically repelled by the notion that someone somewhere might know a fact that I didn't, so I did my best to make sure I had nothing to fear. I studied history and science on my own, pored over atlases memorizing capitals and rivers and mountains, read all the classics.

In third grade our teacher issued a challenge: anyone who could get up in front of the class by the following week and recite the American presidents in order would be awarded a prize.

That was all I needed—a chance to show off and to win a prize doing it! First thing the next morning I reported to the teacher that I was ready. She made the announcement to the class, and I got up and proudly went through the list without hesitation.

The teacher clapped, the kids reluctantly followed suit, and then she gave me an illustrated book on the presidents. I cherished that book. It was a gift that I had earned.

I was sure that no one else in the class was going to try it— at least, I was hoping they wouldn't because that would dilute my accomplishment.

But a few days later Henry got up and did it, and then the following day Laura did, too. They both got their books, just as I had. This was too much. The king of the hill had now become two kings and a queen.

My ego against the wall, I hatched a brilliant plan and rushed home from school that afternoon to work on it. The next day I told the teacher that I could recite the presidents *and their vice-presidents*. The teacher made another announcement, and I got up and rattled them all off without a hitch.

And that ended the game right there. Everyone knew the jig was up. It's a good thing, too, because if someone had gotten up and matched me again, my next move would have been to recite the presidents, vice-presidents, and all their wives, mistresses, children, and pets.

***

Each week we studied ten new vocabulary words. On Fridays the teacher would test us by reciting the words, and we had to write them out on our test papers and use them in sentences.

During the test so many necks were bent at spectacular angles in the attempt to see a neighbor's paper that the classroom looked like a scoliosis clinic.

"Keep your eyes on your own paper," the teacher would intone at regular intervals, without looking up from her desk. It did no good.

In order to keep my answers from going public, I had to hunch over my desk and hide the test with my arms. This was effective, but quite uncomfortable.

Eventually I hit upon a better solution. As the teacher recited the words, I would spell them all incorrectly and then place the test conspicuously at the top of my desk—pretending not to notice all the bulging eyeballs in the immediate area. When the teacher announced that we had only five minutes remaining to complete the test, I would nonchalantly take the paper and, while pretending to review it, correct all the errors.

As far as I know, nobody ever figured out my little game. Or, if they did, they were understandably reluctant to admit it. But if you ever encounter anyone who writes sentences like "He put phuel in his car" or "She ate so much she became obeast," it may be because he sat near me in grade school.

Although I enjoyed my counterespionage exploits, my favorite part of the school day was the recreation period. If we were outdoors we usually played punchball. The rules were similar to baseball, except that the inflatable ball was the size of a basketball and made of soft rubber. The "batter" pitched the ball to himself by throwing it up with one hand and then punching it into the field of play with the other.

There were two standard methods of punching the ball. One was the windmill stroke, where the fully extended arm was swung around like a bat and the ball struck with the thumb side of the fist. This stroke got the greatest distance on the ball, although it ran the risk of the ball being caught on the fly for an easy out; it was used by almost all the boys.

The other method was to slap at the ball with an open hand. The maximum distance obtainable with this technique was about two feet, although it made it impossible to catch the ball for an out. This method was favored by virtually all the girls and one guy, who turned out later in life to be a homosexual.

***

Big Kids were a constant source of stress. They beat us up for no reason. They stole our balls, hats, and books, and played mocking games of catch with them while we stood by helplessly. They knocked our bikes over. They called us names that we didn't even understand.

Big Kids ambushed us between home and school. If we were walking down the sidewalk and saw a group of them coming in our direction, we had to make a choice. We could summon up all our courage and continue walking past them, hoping that our show of nonchalance would disarm them and blunt their attack instinct. On the other hand, by getting so close we presented them with the opportunity to pounce without the inconvenience of a chase.

The alternative was to cross the street. This forced their hand; if they wanted us they had to chase us. The downside was that they may not have wanted us until they saw us cross the street to avoid them.

My earliest fantasies were not of being a star athlete or a spaceman. They involved gaining the strength of Superman so that I could torture and kill Big Kids.

Picture this. I'm walking down the street and here come ten Big Kids, taking up the whole sidewalk. They expect me to cross the street or jump off the curb to let them pass. I just keep walking until we're face to face.

"Excuse me," I say, "I need to get through."

"Say 'pretty please,'" sneers the biggest one.

"Pretty please, you ugly sack of donkey shit," I say, looking up at him.

Shocked into inaction for an instant, the Big Kid recovers and lunges for me. I grab his arm and twirl him screaming around my head like a helicopter blade. Then I let him go and send him flying across the street and through a store window. I make a quick feint toward his friends, who tumble over one another in their haste to escape. I stand there on the sidewalk, doubled over with laughter, as all the bystanders look on in awe.

That was the kind of daydream I had.

Only once did I come close to living out a version of those fantasies. I was walking home from school and a Big Kid named Gene was coming in my direction. He didn't act menacing so I took a chance and passed right next to him. As I did so he reached down and gave me a "noogie," a sharp rap on the top of my head with his knuckles. It hurt so badly that tears literally sprang from my eyes, tears of pain mixed with those of impotent rage.

A child's hate is all-consuming. It can burn for years, as did mine for Gene.

Time passed and I got bigger and stronger, but Gene somehow seemed to stay the same. One day I was in a pickup basketball game on the playground, and Gene was guarding me. He was playing rough and nasty, partially out of clumsiness and partially out of meanness. He finally dug me in the ribs with his elbow, and without thinking I wheeled around and punched him in the stomach. He doubled over and began staggering around in an unsuccessful effort to breathe.

I joyfully watched him struggle for air, and I thought back to the noogie he had administered several years before. He probably didn't even remember doing it. But I had never forgotten it, just as I would never forget that experience of once, just once, feeling a little like Superman.

***

By the time we reached sixth grade we had become Big Kids ourselves. We were the oldest ones in Irving School, the ones on the third floor, and the little kids looked up to and feared us now. (It's amazing how merely staying alive can bestow status.) But this feeling of power was fleeting, since the following year we moved to seventh grade, on the Catskill High School campus. All of a sudden we were little kids again.

The junior high was housed in a wing of the main building, an edifice straight out of a Frank Capra movie: white-columned portico; cascading, stone steps leading to the entrance; ivy-covered walls. The school song was cut from the same cloth:

> In the land of Rip Van Winkle,
> Nestled near the Hudson's shores,
> Stands our dear old Catskill High School,
> Day by day we love thee more.

This was a whole new world! Instead of staying in the same classroom all day with the same boring old teacher, we now moved every hour to a new room and a different boring old teacher. Between classes the halls were filled with hundreds of kids milling about, most of whom we had never seen before. Staying after school was now called "getting detention."

Kids drove to school *in their own cars*, and during lunch hour they gathered in the parking lot drinking sodas, playing the Everly Brothers or Elvis Presley loud on their radios, flirting with the girls. We were introduced to a new species, the "hoods," with ducktail haircuts and leather jackets and taps on the heels of their boots.

This was all heady and intimidating stuff for us born-again little kids.

Around the corner from school was the local hangout, a diner called Jerry's Sugarbowl. It had a dartboard, jukebox and pin-

168

ball machines, hamburgers, fries, and Cokes—all the essentials of teenage life. At lunch and after school the street in front was lined with automotive treasure of all types: 327s, 396s, 427s, two fours, three deuces, Hollies, Hookers, mags, and glasspacks.

People became associated with their "wheels": Wayne was quick off the line, Bobby could lay rubber in fourth, Jimmy could do zero to sixty in 5.8 seconds, Jack blew away a 'Vette last summer across the river.

The local drag strip was a stretch of highway just outside town. Although a two-lane road, it was known as "the four-laners" because it had very wide and smooth shoulders that could easily accommodate a speeding car.

Races took place there most Friday and Saturday nights. Some were impromptu outgrowths of arguments that started in town about whose car was faster, and others were planned for weeks so that at the appointed hour twenty cars were lined up along the side of the road just to watch.

Occasionally the cops showed up and everybody would roar off into the night. Rarely was anyone caught racing, perhaps because the cops weren't trying very hard. And, happily, in all those years there was never a serious accident there.

There were plenty of near misses everywhere else, though, and many of them involved a local hero named Jerry Mack. Jerry was an older kid whose father owned an automobile dealership, and from the time Jerry was old enough to drive he owned and wrecked a limitless series of souped-up automobiles.

One summer afternoon Randy and I were hitchhiking back from Green Lake, a popular swimming spot a few miles outside of town. Jerry picked us up in his latest acquisition and whisked us home at speeds reaching 100 miles an hour on twisty rural roads originally designed for horses and carriages. Randy and I were thrilled to death and scared of dying at the same time.

The next day I opened up the *Daily Mail* and encountered an interesting photo on the front page: it depicted a wrecker pulling a half-submerged car out of Green Lake, with a drenched and bedraggled spectator looking on from shore. Can you guess the name of the spectator? (Answer given below.)

***

In spite of my excitement over my new surroundings, seventh grade dealt me one of the most devastating experiences of my young life: I encountered a course I couldn't handle. In fact, I flunked it. The formal title of this scholastic Waterloo was industrial arts, but everyone just called it "shop."

I had been outraged when I first learned that shop was a required course in junior high school. (The girls had to take homemaking where, presumably, they learned how to clean the houses that the boys learned how to build in shop.) I planned to be a nuclear scientist; I was going to split atoms and put them back together again. And they were going to waste my time teaching me how to pound nails? This was dumb. The Russians were way ahead of us in the space race—were they making their future scientists risk their limbs learning how to use a jigsaw?

Moreover, by the age of thirteen I had already established my terminal hopelessness when it came to tools and machines. I inherited this trait from my father. It's a fact: If your father is handy with tools, so will you be. If not, you end up like me.

If my father had to assemble anything with more than one part, the rest of the family tried to escape the house before the forces of darkness emerged. Screws would break, bolts would strip, pieces would fall on the floor and scurry under the radiator, and the angrier my father got the clumsier he was, and the more determined he became to fix that damned thing even if it killed him.

Sometimes when he had an especially major do-it-yourself project, such as hanging a curtain rod, he'd have me help him, and this is where I learned everything I needed to know to flunk shop.

*Jerry Mack

In fact, I was doomed from the very first day in class when we were introduced to the notion of male and female parts of tools. This was the funniest thing I had ever heard, and any time it was mentioned I would miss the next ten minutes of lecture while I choked down hysterics.

In addition, I'm convinced that, just like animals, inanimate objects can sense when a person is not confident around them and they misbehave accordingly. Otherwise, why could the other students successfully hammer nails into their projects with forceful strokes, laughing and talking while they worked, whereas when I tentatively struck the head of my nail the wood split from end to end?

Why, when we all made simple electric motors by wrapping wire around a rotor and attaching a dry cell battery, did everyone else's project almost take off from the table like a prop jet, while mine sat there like a still life, despite desperate prodding by me and the shop teacher himself? ("Maybe your wire is defective, because everything looks right to me.")

Why was I the only one who was nervous about lighting the gas oven that we used in metal shop, and it was my face it chose to blow up in when it was my turn to light it one day?

No, these were not coincidences. The world of things has tortured me all my life in some sort of diabolical karmic conspiracy. No way was I going to pass shop. No way was I ever going to successfully assemble any kit, or hang any picture, or wash my hands in Chicago's O'Hare Airport.

The airport incident was the glorious culmination of a lifetime of failed efforts at peaceful coexistence with material objects. I had just arrived at O'Hare for a layover after a long flight, and I headed straight for the men's room to "freshen up" (a curious euphemism for pissing and washing your face).

This now was in the 1980s, when progress had eliminated faucet handles on public sinks and paper towels to dry off with. Instead, we now stood passively in front of the sink and let it bestow water upon us at times of its own choosing. Then we punched a button and stood there like idiots trying to dry our hands underneath a mechanically-generated fart. As for drying our faces, we were on our own there. (In desperation, I tried using toilet paper a few times for this purpose, but ended up looking like Santa Claus.)

The airport facility featured a lineup of about ten sinks, and when I entered the room several men were leaning over them, merrily splashing water to their hearts' content. I did my business and then walked over to the first sink and waited. By this time everyone else had left.

No water.

I shoved my hands under the faucet and pretended to wash my hands, figuring that the sink might need more of a hint.

No water.

I moved to the second sink and tried again.

No water.

I banged on the little sensor window to let it know that I meant business.

No water.

I moved to the third sink, then the fourth, and right down the line to the last sink.

No water. Not even a drop from a leaky washer.

By this time two other gentlemen had arrived. I watched as they walked up to the sinks and washed their hands in the abundant streams of water that greeted them as soon as they got to within three feet of the sinks.

When they had gone, I went up to the sinks I had just seen them use. I stood right next to those sinks. I pretended to wash my hands. I banged on those damned little sensor windows with my fist. I called them very bad names.

Nothing.

I started to get dizzy realizing to what great lengths things would go to aggravate me.

And then, in a flash of insight which came as a tremendous relief, I realized what was happening. I was on *Candid Camera*! I expected to see Allen Funt come bursting out of one of the stalls. I really did.

Instead, two airport employees entered the room, one black and one white.

"Can you guys help me?" I asked. "How do you get the damned water to turn on in these sinks?"

It was clear that they thought I must have just come off a long prison stint.

"Oh, those sinks are automatic," said the white guy. "You just have to walk up to the sink and it'll turn on by itself."

To demonstrate, he walked up to one of the sinks and it turned on by itself. I walked up to a sink.

No water.

"Pretend like you're washing your hands. Maybe you're a little too far away."

I pretended I was washing my hands.

No water.

I noticed that the black guy had started to get a weird expression on his face. It was kind of like, well, fearful.

"Here," the white guy said, "come use this one. We know it works."

I walked over to the sink he had just used for his demonstration and waited. I then pretended to wash my hands. I banged on that damned little sensor window.

No water.

The black guy's eyes were now as big as paper plates, and he was backing toward the door.

"No way, Jack, I'm outta' here."

And then he was gone.

The white guy took a few steps back, his eyes never leaving me.

"Look, fella, I don't know what to tell you."

And then he was gone, too. Whatever it was those two had come into the bathroom to do, they didn't do.

There I stood, dry and alone in the middle of an empty men's room in O'Hare Airport. And I knew that, because of me, two more people on earth were now solid believers in the supernatural.

I gave up and walked down the hall until I found another men's room. It looked identical to the first. I tried several sinks with the same lack of results until I finally came to one sink that, when I pretended to wash my hands, would reluctantly choke up a few teaspoons of water at odd intervals. By holding my cupped hands underneath the faucet for minutes at a time I was able to collect enough water to throw on my face.

I will never figure out why that one sink among all the rest took even a little pity on me. My guess is that the sensor was nearsighted and couldn't see that it was me.

But I was stubborn—even into young adulthood I continued to try to fix things. All my friends seemed to be able do that, and some even worked on their own cars. After all, the boys that didn't finish high school all seemed to end up working in garages fixing cars, right? How hard could it be, especially for a smart guy like me?

The first time I resolved to fix something under the hood, I was unable to loosen the bolt. I sprayed on some WD-40 (I was very proud of myself that I knew to do this) and then applied all the force I dared to on the wrench, but it wouldn't break loose. I was afraid to try any harder, for fear of damaging something.

So I gave up, drove the car down to the local garage, and found one of my friends who hadn't finished high school. He put his wrench right where I had put mine and just about stood on it. The bolt came loose.

"You can't be afraid to use a little elbow grease," he said. And I knew he was thinking, *this dumb shit was the valedictorian and he can't even remove a bolt.*

I was embarrassed, but at least I had learned an important lesson: Don't be afraid to use a little elbow grease.

Some months later one of my headlights went out. Well, I wasn't about to pay someone to replace a lousy bulb—I could do it myself. The very first screw I tried to remove from the plastic lens wouldn't budge. I used more force. It wouldn't turn. At this point I normally would have given up for fear of breaking something. But I remembered what I had learned. I applied a little elbow grease.

The plastic lens broke right in half.

I drove the car to the garage and told my friend the story.

"You've got to be careful on a car," he said, "You try to force something and it'll just bite you in the ass." And I knew he was thinking, *this dumb shit was the valedictorian and he can't even change a light bulb.*

That was it for me. I surrendered. I knew then that this dumb shit was fated forever to remain a concept man. Somebody else would have to worry about the nuts and bolts (and charge me dearly for it).

***

So I sailed through junior high school, acing my academic subjects and remaining artless in industrial arts, growing a little taller and buying my first pair of penny loafers.

The big day finally arrived: I started ninth grade. I was now officially a high school student and had all my classes in the main building. But the best thing of all was an absence: NO MORE SHOP!

Instead, a new torture took its place—gym class. I'd always enjoyed that class before. It was the one chance to play during a long and boring school day. But now the equation had changed markedly because of two new factors: Coach Harper and the Big Kids that took gym class with us.

Coach was a small, wiry man of indeterminate age who, soft-spoken though he was, issued directly from the "walk it off" school of physical education. The overriding philosophy here is that real men during recreation should indulge only in physical activities that carry with them a high risk of serious injury, and that when such injury occurs it is incumbent upon the victim to "walk it off."

Fractured ankles? These are walked off. A bloody nose? Tilt your head back and walk it off. A sprained wrist? Hold it over your head and walk it off. Kicked in the groin? Double over if you have to, but keep those legs moving.

Coach delighted in rough play, and his class featured games that were devised by the Marquis de Sade with a migraine. What made it even worse was that gym class was no longer segregated by age. Grades nine through twelve participated in the same class, which meant that we had a range of ages from roughly thirteen to nineteen all trying to prove their manhood to Coach at the same time in the same space. This was like storing dynamite in a foundry.

One of Coach's favorite games was the "crab race." The class was divided into two teams and sent to opposite sides of the gym. A large canvas ball about a yard in diameter was placed at the center circle. When Coach blew his whistle it was a free-for-all, the object being to get the ball to touch the opposing team's wall. The only rule was we had to stay on the floor in a sitting position and move around by walking on all fours, like a crab.

The gym floor quickly became a seething mass of adolescent humanity, with the huge ball bouncing around erratically, sometimes virtually disappearing under a sea of interlocked arms and legs. Heads bounced off the hardwood floor, and wounded participants crawled off to the side to make peace with their pain. They were, of course, instructed to walk it off.

Coach had a bird's-eye view of it all from his standard vantage point up on the bleachers. There he would stand, whistle hanging from his neck, hands clasped behind his back, radiating blissful contentment with the chaos below him.

After a good game of crab, it was time for dodgeball. Again, the class was divided into two teams, each team going to its side of the gym. Then Coach tossed out the dodgeballs, which were smooth, inflated rubber balls about the size of a basketball. The object was to eliminate members of the opposing team by throwing a ball at them and hitting them. If the ball was caught in the air, the thrower was eliminated. The only rule was that players couldn't cross the half-court line. The game ended whenever one team got completely wiped out.

This was essentially the same game we had all been brought up with in elementary school. But with Coach's version we used ten balls instead of two, so that getting creamed by several balls at once was commonplace.

Luckily, the Big Kids usually aimed for one another, but sometimes they decided to pick on a freshman. It was truly pitiful to see a little kid get battered by a well-timed barrage of dodgeballs—especially if that kid was you.

As underclassmen in gym class, our greatest protection was anonymity. We did our best to fade into the background, to avoid doing anything that would attract attention. We didn't want to act like wimps because that was like throwing chum into shark-infested waters. Nor did we want to act too brave. We strived to be the human equivalent of grout.

When class was over, the balls were left behind on the gym floor, and we all marched into the locker room to take our showers and get dressed. This was a most dangerous time for an underclassman because everyone was on an exercise-induced testosterone high, and Coach didn't usually make an appearance for about ten minutes while he collected the gear. Animosities or disagreements sometimes flared up into fights during that ten-minute window of opportunity.

The locker room, with its opaque windows, adjoined the central courtyard around which the school was built. As an example of what terrible things could transpire during shower time, on one occasion an underclassman who had somehow managed to provoke some seniors, probably by looking at them the wrong way, had the misfortune of being tossed bodily out of a locker room window into the central courtyard. Naked.

The window was then locked, leaving the involuntary streaker with absolutely no place to hide from the gaze of several hundred students in the surrounding classrooms. The kid handled it well, under the circumstances; he sat down against a wall and began chewing on a blade of grass in the valiant attempt to make it all look as normal as possible.

A teacher ran down to the locker room and tossed a towel out, and then helped the kid back through the window. The culprits were never caught because no one, including the victim, was willing to turn state's evidence—doing so was an excellent way to attract attention to yourself.

Another time a devious senior smuggled one of the dodgeballs back into the locker room. It got tossed around for a few minutes before fulfilling its date with destiny in the toilet bowl. Without going into detail, suffice it to say that by the end of the day a toilet bowl in a boys' locker room has been ridden hard and put up wet. And there the ball floated, while the kids amused themselves by flushing and watching the ball go through an endless spin cycle.

Eventually Coach arrived, looking for the missing ball. (This reminded me of a mother cat who always seems to know if one of her kittens is missing.) As if by instinct he headed straight for the toilet. I was very curious to see how he was going to fish that ball out. Surely he was going to dress up in a radiation suit and use those remote control tongs. But he didn't hesitate at all. He just reached down, grabbed it, shook it off, and carried it away.

From that day on, playing dodgeball was like playing Russian roulette. Of those ten balls flying around, which was *the one*? Avoiding a direct hit in the face assumed an even greater urgency than usual. After all, a broken nose will heal. But an image can haunt you for life.

Another interesting locker room episode occurred when no one was even in it. On that eventful day we dressed for gym as usual, and Coach secured the locker room behind us as he always did.

When class was over we lined up at the locker room door, waiting for Coach to open it. When he did, a cloud of scalding smoke poured out into the hall, indicating some sort of conflagration within. Coach ran to the nearest fire alarm and tripped it, and the whole school was evacuated to the sound of clanging bells. The common thought among the excited students was similar to that felt on a snowy school night: *Please don't let it stop!*

The firemen arrived within minutes and rushed into the building. When they tried to enter the locker room they, too, were beaten back by the smoke. But they quickly realized that it wasn't smoke at all—it was steam. A fireman donned a protective suit and went in. He found the source of the problem in the shower room: the last kid out of the locker room at the beginning of class had turned on all the showers (there was a bank of at least twenty) to scalding hot, and they had been steaming away for a solid forty-five minutes.

The fireman turned off the showers and opened all the windows, but the locker room was uninhabitable for thirty minutes. We were forced to sit on the bleachers and wait in complete silence. Everyone was looking around, trying to guess the identity of our new hero, looking for a revealing wink or smirk.

Finally we were given the all-clear to go in and change. Just as we were getting dressed a miracle occurred. We were caught in a sudden downpour—indoors! It flashed through my mind that maybe God was punishing us for disrespecting Coach. And maybe He or She was, but the physical fact was that all the moisture that had condensed on the ceiling from the steam had started to come down as if on cue, soaking our already damp clothes.

Once again the culprit was never caught. Everyone in the class had to assemble in the gym after school that day and listen to the principal threaten to keep us until five every afternoon until someone either confessed or was turned in. Neither ever happened, and after a week of mass detention the matter was dropped.

After that incident, the frequency with which we played Coach's favorite game of all seemed to increase. Swat the Fly. That was the name of it.

The rules were elegantly simple. Everybody stood around in a big circle, facing in toward the center, with their eyes closed. The person who was "it" prowled quietly around the outside of the circle, wielding a wide, leather strap supplied by Coach. When he chose his victim, he wound up and whacked him across the rear with the strap.

An intense and sudden pain in the ass was your cue to start running like hell. You ran around the outside of the circle until you got back to your original position. While you were running something very interesting was happening: the guy with the strap was chasing along behind you, flailing away at your backside for all he was worth.

If you were a fast runner you might manage to make it home having suffered only the initial blow. If you were not a fast runner...

It is impossible to forget the feeling of standing with your eyes closed, in a gym filled with echoing silence, and wondering if the sound you were about to hear was that of your own butt getting thrashed. Especially if the guy who was "it" was twice your size and perhaps was someone you had looked at the wrong way somewhere along the line.

(Looking at somebody the wrong way was one of the most common ways of getting in trouble with a Big Kid. Looking at somebody the wrong way could include smiling, sneering, smirking, squinting, frowning, staring, blinking, or winking. It could also include looking at somebody with absolutely no expression at all, or looking the other way—that is, not looking at somebody the wrong way.)

And life holds no feeling of relief quite like standing there with your eyes closed and hearing the sharp crack of the strap and a yelp, and knowing that it wasn't your ass. Then you'd open your eyes so as not to miss a beat and howl with laughter at the cartoon image of a madman with a strap chasing after some poor sucker fleeing to save his hide.

Then that sucker got his turn with the strap and you hoped like hell that he hadn't seen you laughing during his frenzied flight around the circle.

I hated Swat the Fly. The nervous tension involved far outweighed the laughs. How could Coach get away with making us play it? Finally one day Coach came out of his office carrying that damned strap, and I made my stand. I went up to him and, as politely as I could, told him that I wasn't going to play that game anymore. A student, especially a lowly freshman, making that sort of pronouncement to Coach was like one of the disciples begging off from the Last Supper because of a prior engagement.

Coach looked down at me, expressionless.

"Why not, Fried?"

"Because I don't think it's right. It's too easy to get hurt."

I really never expected to get away with this. I anticipated Coach grabbing my arm and pushing me back into place in the Circle of Hell, or dragging me down to the principal for insubordination. No way was Coach going to let a student dictate to him what sorts of character-building activities he was going to participate in.

"Okay, Fried," he said softly, "You go over there and sit on the bleachers and watch."

I couldn't believe it. It was too easy. Something definitely was wrong.

"Is there anyone else here who thinks this game is a little too rough for them?" boomed the Coach as I headed for the bleachers. "If so, go over there and sit with Fried."

So there it was. The Coach had pulled the trump card of coaches and drill sergeants everywhere—the public pansy insinuation. If you want to get a male to do something against his will and all else has failed, try suggesting that maybe, just maybe, he's a little too delicate for the job. He'll bite the head off a chicken. Run headlong into a hail of bullets. Swat that fly for all he's worth.

A handful of other delicate types broke from the circle and joined me on the bleachers. The Insurrection of the Pansies was growing! And then a few more trickled over.

Left on the floor were those few who truly enjoyed the game, and the rest who would have gladly joined us on the bleachers but who could not overcome Coach's psychological weapon.

There we were, a microcosm of society: the orchestrating political power, the gung-ho believers, the reluctant soldiers, and over there on the bleachers the fringe element who, for better or worse, threatened the stability of it all.

The game went on that day, but something had clearly changed in the balance of power. After that, we never played Swat the Fly again. Coach must have suspected that if it came to a showdown involving the administration, he wouldn't win.

The pansies had overcome!

***

In spite of a strong instinct to rebel against what I perceived to be authoritarian irrationality (and I perceived it everywhere), I managed to stay out of serious trouble in school. But in tenth-grade biology class I got the scare of my life.

As part of our final grade we had to do a class project. We had a choice: we could work alone and write a paper on some topic in biology, or we could team up with someone and conduct and document a biology experiment of our own design.

I had always been fascinated by the topic of suspended animation, where a cold-blooded animal can actually become frozen in ice and yet still survive. I shared my interest with my friend Paul, and he said that there was a pond in the woods near his house that was full of frogs. Why couldn't we use them for an experiment on suspended animation?

It seemed perfect. Naturally, we left everything until the last weekend before the project was due. That Sunday I trooped up to Paul's house, and we grabbed some sacks and headed into the woods toward the pond.

The pond was postcard beautiful, sprinkled with lily pads and shaded by overhanging boughs of willows. It was enough to bring tears to your eyes. However, the tears in our eyes were caused by the fact that there was not one frog to be seen. Maybe it was the wrong season. Or maybe they had heard about our experiment and the whole concept of being suspended animatedly left them cold.

Whatever it was, without those frogs Paul and I were screwed. Too little time remained to take the other option and do individual research papers, and we could think of no other possible experiment to perform on such short notice. We walked back to the house in sickened silence, Paul cursing me under his breath for getting him into this mess, and I cursing Paul under mine for not checking out the frog situation sooner.

It all seemed hopeless. But necessity is a mother, and soon I had devised an ingenious plan. We would do the whole experiment in our heads and then write it up as real.

Now some might call this cheating. But ample precedence for it can be found in the annals of science. Albert Einstein became famous for his thought experiments on the relativity of space and time. Why couldn't we do it with frozen frogs?

Paul, having little choice, agreed to go along with it. So we sat at his kitchen table and constructed the whole fiction, using beautifully drawn charts and colored timelines.

Frog #1:
Put frog in freezer for five minutes and removed.
His reaction time seemed normal. Slapped ruler
on table, and he jumped immediately.
Frog #2:
Put frog in freezer for ten minutes and removed.
Reactions were sluggish. Jumped weakly when
we slapped the table with ruler. After ten min-
utes at room temperature, reactions normal.

And so it went, right up to the frog that we kept in the freezer for five hours and then tried to thaw out. We didn't want to push our luck too far, so this unfortunate frog died.

Then we tied it all together with some theories and conclusions, put it in a leather-covered binder, and the next day we burned all our bridges and handed it in.

For the next few weeks we lived in fear. Would Mr. Mansfield, our teacher, easily recognize what we had done? Did we make some obvious blunder that gave it all away? What would happen if we were found out? With this on our records we'd never get into college. Our parents would cut off our allowances for life. We might even make the front page of the *Daily Mail*. Our whole lives were hanging in the balance.

Finally Mr. Mansfield announced at the beginning of a class that he had completed grading the projects, that he was proud of most of us, but disappointed in the efforts of a few. Paul and I stared down at our desks. In which camp were we?

Then Mr. Mansfield walked around the room and handed out the papers—all except ours. He returned to the front of the classroom and, in an eerily even tone, intoned those magic words, "Denny and Paul, please see me after class."

Yep, no doubt about it, we were definitely going for a ride down Shit Creek in a leaky boat. For the remainder of the hour I sat there and pretended to take notes, while I wrestled with my stomach over the issue of throwing up.

The longest biology class in recorded history eventually ended, and Paul and I dutifully trudged up to Mr. Mansfield's desk. I was hoping I looked at least a little better than Paul, whose face was so white he could have attended a Klu Klux Klan rally without the hood.

"Denny, Paul, I have been a teacher for thirty years."

Oh, man, I thought, *are we screwed.*

"And in that time I have had some very good moments, when teaching was a pure joy, and some very terrible moments, when I wondered why I stayed in the profession."

I'll never be able to look at my parents again.

"But in all that time, I have never had any of my students turn in a research project as ..."

Can I make it to Mexico on three dollars?

" . . . original and well done as yours."

HOLY SHIT, WE DID IT!

"And I'd like your permission to enter it in a nationwide science contest."

HOLY SHIT, WHAT DO WE DO NOW? WHAT IF WE WIN?

"That would be fine, sir," we agreed modestly. Then we gathered our books, left the classroom, and made a beeline for the nearest exit. As soon as we got outside we slumped down on the grass, emotionally exhausted from the gauntlet of emotions we had just run.

"Man, I hope we don't win that thing," said Paul.

"Hey, maybe it wouldn't be too bad."

"Yeah, maybe you're right. That paper is damned good."

Then we lay back and laughed ourselves sick.

Several months later Mr. Mansfield sadly reported that he had received the contest results. We weren't among the winners. We hadn't even received an honorable mention.

Paul and I were outraged. After all, that paper was damned good.

9

Girls

Like all well-adjusted males, my friends and I spent the first ten
years of our lives avoiding girls at all costs (in sharp contrast to
the rest of our lives, where girls were pursued regardless of cost).

The simple truth was that, at that age, girls had nothing of
interest to offer. They seemed to do everything in slow motion,
and they often cried for no discernible reason. We couldn't swear
in front of them, or they'd run home and tell their mothers, and
then they would call our mothers, and then we could kiss our
allowance good-bye for a while. And they had no toys that any
self-respecting boy would be caught dead in the same room with.

So what was the point?

Worst of all, they were totally inept at sports. In our elementary school years, when the weather was rainy or cold our daily
recreation period was held in the gym. This was where we received our early training in dodgeball; and, because of its nature, the boys played separately from the girls.

The boys played hard and fast. It was not uncommon to be
left with a red welt when hit with the ball. Strategy was employed. If a team managed to collect both balls at the same time,
the two throwers would move up to the half-court line to get as
close to the enemy as possible, while the other team cowered
against the back wall. A target was agreed upon and then both

throwers would launch at the same time, one aiming for the head and the other for the groin. In the form of play, we were learning skills that would be invaluable in adulthood.

The boys' game was over in ten minutes because it is nearly impossible to protect your head and your balls at the same time. Then we'd have to sit down while the girls played. This was like watching rock erode in slow motion. First of all, girls do not really want to hit each other with a ball; unlike boys, for whom it is a natural instinct, the notion of aiming a projectile at another living thing in order to eliminate it from consideration is completely foreign to them.

Secondly, in those days when a thrown object left a girl's hand it usually did not go in the direction dictated by science. Rather, it flew out at an impossible angle that defied the laws of motion. The result was that the girls were just as likely to hit their own teammates, or the spectators, as members of the opposing team.

So there we boys would sit for the next thirty minutes, anxious to play again and dying from frustration as the girls wafted balls aimlessly at the floor, walls, and ceiling.

Then the period would be over, with both of the girls' teams still at full strength, and we were marched back to the classroom, knowing that we would have to wait another whole day before we'd get our next ten minutes of sanctioned fun.

But in spite of my instinctive aversion to girls, I managed to have my first sexual experience when I was in the second grade, although I didn't know it at the time. And to this day, neither does the young lady I had it with.

Her name was Valerie Brown, and she appeared mysteriously one day in our small, second-grade classroom, and she disappeared just as mysteriously at the end of the school year. I never saw her again.

I do not remember ever speaking a word to her. Of course, this was normal: no seven-year-old male would voluntarily talk to a girl unless she was an adult, a family member, or had some leftover Halloween candy.

Nor do I remember ever looking at Valerie Brown and thinking strange or unusual thoughts. The notion of feminine beauty or sensuality just was not yet a part of my conceptual framework.

But one night I had a dream about Valerie Brown.

It was a blue-sky summer day. And Valerie Brown and I were alone and swimming lazily around a big pool, long, slow strokes, around and over and under each other, never actually touching, not talking, just moving effortlessly in each other's presence through the cool water's caress. There was a feeling to it, a very vague, pleasurable feeling that had nothing to do with the swimming and everything to do with Valerie Brown.

I woke up not understanding this dream at all. With a pool like that, I could have had all my friends over and played raft tag or splash the monster. What had I been doing there with Valerie Brown? A girl.

When I got to school that morning I was too embarrassed to even look at Valerie Brown. The dream had been so vivid and real that I felt that somehow she must know it, too. And when, at last, our eyes finally met for a fleeting moment, I felt that she was looking directly into a part of me that even I did not understand.

For the rest of that school year I could not look at Valerie Brown without feeling vulnerable, without feeling that somehow my own expression was betraying my dark secret. Whatever it was.

The school year ended, summer came and went, and when classes started again Valerie Brown was gone. I knew that because I made it a point to look for her the first day in all the third-grade classes.

And that was my introduction to the adult pastime of loving and losing.

***

I was ten years old when my father got trapped into telling me the facts of life.

It wasn't that we kids were completely unaware of strange goings-on between men and women. For example, in third grade we were studying American humor, and each of us had to learn a representative joke and tell it to the class. Eddie, a very bright black kid who was also extremely dizzy, got up and told his:

Flo, the Reverend's wife, knocked on the front door, and little Bessie answered.

"Bessie, is your mama home?"

"Yes'm, Miss Flo, but she upstairs all laid up with arth-r-itis."

"Mercy sakes, child, I know them Ritus boys and that Arthur is the worsest one!"

Poor Eddie paid a visit to Mrs. Avery, and so did his mother.

As time went on, my knowledge of the sex act itself got even more detailed by listening to the Big Kids tell dirty jokes under the apple tree in the playground. But as far as I could determine, only the most perverted, sick, and lowdown people in the world did it, such as traveling salesmen and farmers' daughters.

One night my father and I were alone in the house watching *Medic*, one of the first of the doctor shows on television. The story that evening involved a young couple who wanted to have a baby but were having no luck. So they went to the doctor (played by Richard Boone) to find out what was wrong.

Everything made perfect sense to me, until it came time for the conference in the doctor's office. The doctor was telling the man that something was wrong with *him*!

What could that possibly have to do with the woman not being able to have a baby?

"Dad," I said, "I don't understand this show."

"What don't you understand about it?"

"Well, the woman can't have a baby, but the doctor's saying that something is wrong with the man."

My father was caught between the desire to educate his child and the fear of teaching a seminar for which he was unprepared.

"Keep watching, maybe it will all make sense to you in a little while," he stalled.

So I kept watching, but it didn't help one bit. Now the doctor was giving the man all kinds of tests and even talking about surgery, while his wife who couldn't have a baby was merrily chatting it up in the waiting room.

"Dad, this doesn't make any sense."

My father now had little choice.

"Do you know how a woman has a baby?" he asked.

"Well, when she gets to a certain age she just starts having them." (This was my "apple tree" theory of human procreation.)

"Well, that's true, a woman does need to reach a certain age, but there's more to it than that. The man has to do something, too, to start the baby."

He stopped there, probably hoping that now the truth would be revealed to me without his having to help it along any further.

"Huh?"

"Well, the woman carries an egg inside her, which has to be fertilized by the man in order to start a baby."

This was starting to have a disgusting ring to it.

"Huh?"

"The man has to put his penis inside the woman in a place between her legs, and a seed comes out and fertilizes the egg."

And with those words the world as I knew it went directly to hell in a bullet train.

"Oh, no!" I moaned. I felt sick right down to my core.

"What's the matter?" my father asked.

"THAT'S CALLED FUCKING!" I screamed.

Now it was my father's turn to show emotional distress.

"Where did you learn that?"

"From the Big Kids on the playground. They talk and tell jokes about it."

I was almost in tears. The implications were crashing into my consciousness like waves:

(1) It wasn't just traveling salesmen and farmers' daughters!

(2) Every person in the world represents two people doing it!

(3) My very own parents had done it twice!

(4) I'd probably have to do it myself someday!

I couldn't believe that my own parents could have gotten mixed up in something like this.

"But who'd want to do that?" I was desperate for my father to tell me something that would make it all comprehensible.

"When you get older you'll understand. When you fall in love with someone it will just be something that you'll want to do."

I was clinically depressed for a week. The whole world seemed like a traitorous place to me, not to be trusted any longer. What else might be going on out there—maybe in my own house even—that I wasn't supposed to understand until I got older?

But ever so gradually I started getting used to the idea. Eventually it didn't all seem quite so revolting. It even started to seem, well, interesting.

And, ultimately, I grew very proud of my newfound knowledge. I told all my friends the truth about babies. I even told a girl in my class whom I found, well, interesting.

***

Some time after that I was riding my bike on the outskirts of town when I spotted a magazine page lying in the weeds. I hit the brakes and fetched it.

One side of the page featured a photo of a beautiful lady. She was dressed like a cowgirl. That is, she was wearing a western hat and a holster and nothing else. She was standing haughtily facing the camera, with shapely slender legs spread apart. Long black hair poured down from underneath the hat, framing huge, perfectly round breasts. (The holster, unfortunately, was turned around in front so as to cover up the other area of extreme interest.)

And it was at that precise moment that finally, finally I became old enough to understand.

My father was right.

When you fall in love with someone it's just something that you want to do.

10

Time to Go

Kids are always impatient to get older, because it seems to them that they are merely marking time until they can drive, drink, date, and leave home—at which time, of course, life becomes absolutely carefree and perfect.

Once those milestones are reached, however, the advantages of continuing to age become much harder to identify. Like any long-term project, each one of us at some point goes from the research and development stage to that of maintenance and repair, and the former tends to be a lot more fun.

We all have unforgettable moments (which we would like to forget) when we realize that physically we are not what we used to be. I can recall two very clear instances in my own life.

My friends and I used to climb up a stone wall to get onto the roof of my house. Then we would stand on the edge of the roof and jump as far as we could onto the grassy slope about eight feet below. The object was to see who could land the farthest away from the house. Sometimes we even wore capes, or constructed crude wings out of sheets, but nothing that we tried seemed to have any effect on our airtime.

None of us ever got hurt doing this. We'd hit the ground and then roll like we saw the paratroopers do in the movies. We wished the roof was even higher so we could fly further.

Years later, I was home from college on summer vacation when our roof developed a leak. I volunteered to go up to see if I could locate the source of the problem. I managed, with only a little difficulty, to climb up the wall as I had done so many times before and check out the roof. (Of course, I didn't find anything helpful; I didn't expect to. What I was doing was merely token behavior, similar to opening the hood of the car when it fails to start.)

Now the problem was to get back down. I had assumed on the way up that I'd descend as I always had, by jumping. I began to question this assumption as soon as I got to the edge of the roof and peered down. Something had changed, because it seemed to me now that I was looking down from the Empire State Building. And I realized, with some surprise, that if I was honest with myself I'd have to admit that no way in hell did I *want* to jump off that roof.

I considered other options. I could try to climb back down the stone wall, but getting in position to start the climb down would be risky, and I'd never done that before. I could also try to hang off the roof by my hands and drop to the ground that way, but I was sure that I'd get all scraped up in the process.

I came up with a compromise (a very adult thing to do). I sat on the edge of the wall and pushed myself off, thereby reducing by a few feet the height of my fall.

I hit the ground and stuck there, like a sack of moldy cheese. I felt as though my legs had been driven right up through my chest. Every bone in my body vibrated and all my internal organs were sloshing around like water balloons. I sat down in the grass and tried to remember the trick to inhaling air, something which at that moment had escaped me, along with all my breath.

This episode depressed me no end. It was the first time in my life that I was forced to recognize that something had been lost physically. In fact, this was so hard for me to accept that over the next few days I thought about going back up and trying it again, on the theory that I had just had the misfortune of landing wrong.

But I didn't.

The second incident took place when I was in my thirties. A friend had bought a speedboat and invited me to go out on the river with him. I thought this would be great fun, because like most males I'd always enjoyed the sensation of speed and the frisson of risk that goes along with it.

The water was rough, the wind was strong. We bounced along at high speed, the sun and spray in my face, the wind in my hair. The mountains loomed in the distance and the intoxicating smell of pine permeated the air. Who could ask for anything more?

I could and did—I asked my friend to slow down and deliver me back to solid ground. I had enjoyed as much of that bouncing up and down on a hard seat as I could stand. My stomach felt like it had cut loose from its usual moorings and was wandering around looking for a safe place to hide. Twenty years earlier I would have been badgering my friend to take us faster. Now all I wanted to do was sit on a nice, stationary beach chair and watch *him* go faster.

There are some other signs of getting older you should watch for. For example, it's a bad sign when you stop listening to Top Forty radio because all the music on it is crap.

If you're male, another good indicator is which family member you find yourself lusting after in TV commercials. It starts with the daughter. Then at some point you realize that the mother is the real dish. If you live long enough, the grandmother's sparkling white hair and bright red cheeks strike you as kind of sexy. And if you really live long enough, you're drooling over the daughter again.

In my youth, I wondered why old people always had so many things wrong with them. Now I know. When you're young, injuries and illnesses come and go. When you're not, injuries and illnesses come and stay.

I've noticed another interesting phenomenon associated with aging. When I was a child my father would sometimes forget whether a certain movie star had died or not. He'd ask my mother and she very often couldn't remember, either.

I couldn't at all comprehend not remembering if a famous person had died. I certainly recalled all the well-known people who had died during *my* lifetime. Death was of such terrifying magnitude that, to me, not being able to remember if Gary Cooper had died would be like forgetting that he had grown a second head.

Then, at some point in my life, the same thing started happening to me. I'd read about the death of a movie star I'd grown up watching, like Burt Lancaster, and it would sadden me considerably. I'd think about his movies that I had enjoyed, perhaps recalling where and with whom I was when I saw them.

A year later I'd see Burt Lancaster in a movie on TV and wonder if he was still alive.

The difference, of course, is that when we are young death is still a rarity. It likely hasn't touched our family or friends (yet), and we haven't been around long enough to have lost many of our favorite celebrities. Death is still a terrible stranger, one whose visits cannot be forgotten. To the young, not only is the person destroyed by death, but to a large extent their very concept of that person is irretrievably altered as well.

As we get older and death becomes more commonplace, it becomes less destructive of our concept of the person. It's easier for us to think of a departed friend without death being an essential part of our mental image. It becomes easier for us to think of a movie star and not remember if she has died.

In some "primitive" cultures deceased members are considered as much a part of the community as living ones. There, in a very real sense, death is just another stage of citizenship. This seems to me a very enlightened perspective—perhaps a sign of a very old culture, as opposed to a very young one.

Most of us are afraid of dying, or at least don't want to do it anytime soon. We know that death is inevitable, as long as it's Not In My Back Yard.

This is why I've known since I was a child exactly what I want on my epitaph—no date after the dash.

Perhaps Woody Allen put it best: "I don't want to be immortal through my work—I want to be immortal through not dying."

We don't want to die, but would we choose to live forever? What kind of music would they play at our 1000th high school reunion?

***

Age is reputed to bring wisdom. I'm still waiting.

But I have learned a few things worth sharing:

- People who have the most to say usually have the least to offer and are the least likely to act.

- People lie, exaggerate, and err more than you might imagine. Keep this in mind before you let something someone says affect your emotional life too seriously.

- Your life will not turn out the way you think. It is the height of arrogance to expect that you have enough control over the universe to shape your future to meet your expectations.

- The most worthless commodity in the world is other people's opinions.

- The reality of a career is very different from your image of it.

- A false start or a failure is not a waste of time—it is an essential part of the process.

- Success requires that you begin, which is very difficult. It also requires that you persist, which is even more difficult, because it is like having to begin over and over again.

- The gurus of positive thinking often claim that you can achieve anything you want if you work hard enough. Unfortunately, this is nonsense and the cause of much self-deprecation.

Wanting something badly and working hard for it gives you a chance, not a guarantee.

- Most "accidents" that we have are perfectly predictable. In fact, our inner voice often warns us but we ignore it. As we start climbing up the shaky ladder, the voice tries to tell us to get back down and reposition it, but we're in too much of a hurry. As we start to slice the apple on a wet plate, the voice urges us to get the cutting board, but we decide to cut just a little more carefully instead. After we break our hips and mutilate our fingers, we totally forget that we had been warned. Listen to your inner voice—it will save you some bloodshed, and maybe your life.

- Within all of us exists constant warfare between two basic instincts: the instinct for security and comfort and that for adventure. For some the battle is overwhelmingly one-sided: people whose entire lives are dominated by the need for security and comfort. Travel to a foreign country is out of the question. Going to the mall is an epic journey. Some never learn to drive. Some never leave their homes. At the other end of the scale are those who die at age twenty-five from falling off a frozen mountain in Nepal.

In most of us this battle is more evenly fought. By age thirty-five I had spent the first half of my life dedicated primarily to intellectual endeavors, my adventures largely confined to the cloisters of the conceptual realm.

I was tired of thinking, tired of the constant struggle to be clever and bright. Instead of reflecting on the world, I now wanted to immerse myself in it, to feel it.

I took up whitewater canoeing. In spite of my terror of flying, I took glider lessons. Having never camped out a day in my life, I embarked on an extremely arduous two-week, guided canoe trek in the Canadian Northwoods. And, with a smattering of Spanish, I got in my ten-year-old beater of a car and drove to Mexico to roam for the winter.

Driving alone through the hinterlands of Mexico is not for the fainthearted. The roads are horrendous, the drivers worse, the police unpredictable, and bandits commonplace. After a week of rough travel and spartan lodging, I landed in a rather nice motel in a small city. The shower had hot water and the room was clean. My car was safely parked. I got to know the young desk clerk, and he recommended a neighborhood restaurant for dinner. I walked to it and had a terrific meal, while the friendly staff encouraged my poor Spanish.

I intended to resume my journey the following day, but when I woke I felt so comfortably weary and content that I decided that I needed another day of relaxing before hitting the road again. I spent the day exploring the city and studying Spanish; I joked with the desk clerk about women, and I had dinner again at my usual haunt.

The next morning I lay in bed and had an argument with myself. I knew it was time to move on; I had seen what there was to see and given myself a chance to recharge. But I felt so comfortable, at peace and secure. I had made some friends, knew my way around. In two days I had made myself a nest—I had gone from the tightrope of the road to the predictability of a home.

Never before had I felt the elemental battle of the instincts played out so clearly in the open. Facing the risks, discomforts, and unknowns of the road required energy; it was exhilarating, but wearing. I could stay in the motel for the rest of the winter, have a hot shower and clean sheets every day. I wouldn't have to worry about car trouble, or the police, or highway robbery.

But complacent comfort was exactly what I had come to Mexico to escape: it is extremely seductive, but to abandon yourself to it for the long haul means coloring your life with a meager palette.

Managing to overcome an extreme inertia, I packed up my things and said good-bye to my friend at the front desk. I got out my map and followed the desolate highway west out of town, toward the Sierra Madre mountains. A tumbleweed blew into the road and got caught momentarily in the grill of my car. Then it broke free and careened off into the desert, as if late for an appointment.

It made me laugh, and I was happy.

***

Yes, you can go home again—back to where it was, but not to what it was.

I went back to where it was for a single day a few years ago, at the end of a business trip north.

As I approached Catskill in my rented car, I rounded a curve and the mountains appeared before me exactly as they had so many times before. But this time tears sprang into my eyes, driven by emotions I didn't know I had. I grew up in the shadow of those glacier-molded hills. They were the ever-present backdrop to the first half of my existence, and they are in my soul in a way landscapes adopted later in life can never be.

I drove slowly down Main Street, peering through the windshield as if at a museum exhibit: rows of boarded-up stores where honest commerce used to be; dust and garbage swirling down the mostly deserted sidewalks; a faded mural on a building wall of Mike Tyson, Catskill's favorite son, who was now serving time for rape.

I saw an old man sitting in front of the firehouse. I was startled to recognize him as the young man that used to sit there when I was a kid.

I stopped in front of Andy's house. The neat, white house I remembered was now peeling and frayed—Sam would hate that.

I walked down the street to the apartments of Irwin and Tommy, and entered the dingy alley over which they had constructed their ill-fated telephone network. The alley seemed narrower and shorter than my recollection of it, but at least it smelled the same—cats.

A few more paces up Main Street and now I was standing in front of my house. I looked up at the big, plate glass window behind which my father had drilled and pulled so many teeth (including mine), slowly destroying his health in the struggle to provide for his family. Another dentist was in there now. Since my father's death more than thirty years ago there has been a long succession of dentists up there. Perhaps a dental office can never be anything else.

I walked around to the back of the building. The gate into the yard where we had played out our childhood fantasies was chained and locked. The evergreen trees that had ringed our property were gone. Everything seemed so much smaller than I remembered. I wondered if Sardo still had some bones buried there.

I walked to the Irving School. At least that looked much the same. Were students still being sent to see Mrs. Avery? And there was the playground. The hill where we spent so many happy hours sledding was completely eroded at its base and overgrown with weeds and brush. Where did the kids sled now? Or did they now just play a sledding game on their computers? Maybe that's better—they stay warm and dry, and they can just zap the Big Kids with a ray gun.

I sat in a swing for the first time in decades, remembering how we used to swing so high we thought we would go right over the top. I lifted my feet off the ground and gave a half-hearted pump with my legs. Up and back I went, and then I stopped myself short and jumped off before I got sick.

Slightly dizzy, I went back to the car. I drove past the high school (the scene of several violent racial clashes in recent years) and on to Leeds. Most of the resorts that had lined the way were gone: some had been converted to private residences, and others were now simply overgrown fields with no trace of buildings or the joy that had animated them.

Only two bars remained in Leeds, and O'Shea's now featured heavy metal bands. Just down the street was Slippery Rock. It was completely fenced in and obscured by tall weeds, with NO TRESPASSING signs posted every few yards.

I walked onto the old stone bridge that crossed over the creek to get a better view. The rocky shore that led down to the water looked the same. I guess rock was one thing you could count on, unless it got blasted away to put in a new highway. But the water was filthy, covered with streaky residue and rust-colored foam along the edges.

It's all gone totally and directly to hell, I thought. What lousy luck to get stuck in a universe where time tends to make things worse instead of better. Catskill was still a small town, but all the advantages were gone. No Catskill kids were ever again going to enjoy the kind of childhood I had.

Perhaps no kids anywhere were.

I spent the rest of the day on frenzied visits to friends and relatives. It has always amused me that when I don't see friends for a week I have a million things to tell them; but when I don't see them for years, "everything is fine" just about covers it.

Very early the next morning I drove to the Albany airport and boarded my flight. We took off and made a sweeping turn south, and as we were still gaining altitude we passed almost directly over Catskill: Main Street, the schools, Lee Brown's Cherry Farm, Leeds—all receding slowly below me, framed by the blue of the river and the green of the mountains. It all looked perfect again—I guess altitude and time both play the same tricks.

A few hours later we descended through the cloud cover. I looked down to see the Gulf lapping at sand so white it hurt the eyes, golf courses and orange-tiled roofs stretching to the horizon, palm-lined streets and shopping malls.

I was home again.

About the Author

Dennis Fried is the author of the popular *Memoirs of a Papillon: The Canine Guide to Living with Humans without Going Mad* (www.dogtellsall.com). He holds advanced degrees in physics and philosophy, and has been laughed out of numerous careers, including that of college teaching, marketing, software development, and stand-up comedy. He lives in Sarasota, Florida, with his wife, Katrina, and their adopted four-legged daughter, Genevieve.